rather_san francisco_

eat. shop. explore > discover local gems

researched, photographed and written by kaie wellman

toc

neighborhoods

EAT

à côté
adesso
bar agricole
bar bambino
bar jules
benkyodo
boccalone
boot and shoe service
brown sugar kitchen
bun mee
camino
chilango
contigo
dynamo donuts + coffee
flour + water
frances
il cane rosso
jai yun
la palma mexicatessen
lers ros
little skillet
little vine
local 123
miette pâtisserie & confiserie
mission chinese food
moscow and tbilisi bakery
namu
nopalito
outerlands
plow
sandbox bakery
sebo
sightglass coffee
singapore malaysian
smitten ice cream
spqr
taste
tcho
vintage berkeley
wexler's

SHOP

acrimony
basil racuk
battersea
bell'occhio
birch
candystore collective
cask
clary sage organics
conifer
eden & eden
esqueleto
general store
gravel & gold
gypsy honeymoon
ichiban kan
jak horne
japan woodworker
lotus bleu
mac
mcmullen
mercy vintage now
modern relics
nest
nomade exquis
oak barrel winecraft
omnivore books on food
pot + pantry
press: works on paper
rare device
reliquary
story boxes
talisman antiques
taylor stitch
the bone room
the brooklyn circus
the curiosity shoppe
the gardener
the perish trust
timeless treasures
tradesmen
twig & fig
unionmade

notes
about
san francisco

rather *san francisco* EDITOR >

Kaie Wellman is the creator of the *eat.shop guides* and *rather*. She likes nothing better than traipsing around a city peering into its nooks and crannies. though a lover of pretty objects and fine food, Kaie loves puffy down vests and donuts.

Though I don't like to play favorites, I do love working on this particular title. Wandering around San Francisco and the East Bay on a warm, sun-filled day, where everything seems touched by gold and the bay sparkles—there's nowhere else like it. It's on these days that even when I'm circling for a parking spot for the 15th time, my love for the city stays intact.

Though lots of ground is covered in this book, one area that's not covered is the ever-growing food cart scene—so here's a bit of information for your exploring purposes. You can follow @streetfoodsf on Twitter to get some ideas or www.sfcartproject.com for schedules. Here are some of my recommendations: Creme Brulee Cart (@cremebruleecart), Soul Cocina (@soulcocina), Gobba Gobba Hey (@gobbagobbahey), Toasty Melts (@toastymelts), Roli Roti (@roliroti) and Who's Your Daddy Bacon Potato Chips (@baconpotatochip), 4505 Meat (@4505.Meats).

Finally, If you find yourself in need of a some downtime from eating and shopping, here are some suggestions outside of that realm:

1 > The Audium: A place defined as an exploration of space in music, where aural sculptures are created. A one-of-a-kind SF experience.

2 > Yerba Buena Center for the Arts: Contemporary art has a hold on SF, and Yerba Buena is a great place to experience cutting-edge exhibitions and performances. It's also conveniently across the street from SFMoma, which is always a must visit.

3 > Walking over the Golden Gate Bridge: No joke, it's a breath-taking experience.

3 > Taking a Drive: Okay, this is out of San Francisco, but it's a gorgeous drive. Take 101 north and exit on Highway 1 as it heads west through Muir Woods up to Point Reyes.

it's all about...

exploring locally

*discovering a sense of place
behind the veneer of a city*

*experiencing what gives
a city its soul through its
local flavor*

rather EVOLUTION

If you are thinking that this book looks suspiciously like an *eat.shop guide*, you're on to something. As of October 2011, the *eat.shop guides* evolved into **rather** to give readers a more vibrant experience when it comes to local eating and shopping. It's all about what you'd **rather** be doing with your time when you explore a city—eat at a chain restaurant or an intimate little trattoria devouring dishes the chef created from farm fresh ingredients? You get the idea.

USING **rather**

All of the businesses featured in this book are first and foremost locally owned, and they are chosen to be featured because they are utterly authentic and uniquely conceived. And since this isn't an advertorial guide, there's no money exchanging hands • Make sure to double check the hours of the business before you go, as many places change their hours seasonally • The pictures and descriptions for each business are meant to give a feel for a place, but please know those items may no longer be available • Our maps are stylized, meaning they don't show every street • Small local businesses have always had to work that much harder to keep their heads above water, and not all the businesses featured will stay open. Please go to the **rather** website for updates • **rather** editors research, shoot and write everything you see in this book • Only natural light is used to shoot and there's no styling or propping

restaurants >
$ = inexpensive $$ = medium $$$ = expensive

Go to **rather.com** to learn more

where to
lay your
weary head

for more hotel choices, visit >

HotelSanfrancisco.com

TravelShark

PART OF THE TRAVELSHARK
GLOBAL NETWORK

joie de vivre hotels
800.738.7477 / jdvhotels.com
standard double from $100
notes: there are 18 affordable, well-conceived
and executed jdv boutique properties in sf and
the east bay.
favorites: hotel tomo (funky, bright, japanese),
good hotel (urban simplicity with a green edge)
and hotel vitale (modern luxe with glorious views
of the bay)

crescent hotel
417 stockton street (union square)
415.400.0500 / crescentsf.com
standard double from $160
notes: where modern and classic meet

hotel palomar
12 fourth street (financial district)
415.348.1111 / hotelpalomar-sf.com
standard double from $170
restaurant: the fifth floor
notes: urban luxury in the center of the action

hotel frank
386 geary street (union square)
415.986.2000 / hotelfranksf.com
standard double from $240
restaurant: max's on the square
notes: retro glam

cavallo point lodge
601 Murray Circle - Fort Baker (sausalito)
415.339.4700 / cavallopoint.com
historic queen from $290
contemporary queen from $ 240
restaurant: murray circle restaurant, farley bar
notes: stay across the bay from the city in either
a historic or a contemporary room

more eating gems

these businesses appeared in
previous editions of eat.shop san francisco

EAT

24th street cheese co.
a16
anthony's cookies
aziza
bakesale betty
bar crudo
bar tartine
bi-rite creamery
biondivino
blue bottle coffee
bob's donuts
bocadillos
bombay ice creamery
boulette's larder
bourbon and branch
canteen
canyon market
cam huong
césar
cheese plus
chocolate covered
coi
crixa cakes
dosa
emmy's spaghetti shack
essencia
farmer brown
ferry building farmers market
four barrel coffee
gialina
guerilla cafe
hotel biron
humphrey slocombe
ici
la taqueria
liguria bakery
lovejoy's tea room
lucca delicatessen
mission pie
nopa
on the bridge
piccino
pizzaiolo
pizzeria delfina
pizzetta 211
range
ritual coffee
rosamunde sausage grill
saigon sandwiches
sam's grill

seasalt
shanghai dumpling king
sociale
sophia cafe
spork
st. francis fountain
stella pasticceria
summer kitchen bakeshop
swan oyster depot
tadich grill
tamarindo
tartine bakery
thanh thanh cafe
the alembic
the blue plate
the candy store
the front porch
tokyo fish
true burger
true sake
underdog
vik's chaat corner
walzwerk
weirdfish
yank sing
zante pizza
zuni cafe

more shopping gems

these businesses appeared in previous editions of eat.shop san francisco

SHOP

826 valencia
addison endpapers
al's attire
alla prima
arch
aria
article pract
atys
belljar
carrots
cactus jungle
cookin'
creativity explored
cris
dandelion
dema
delilah crown (now gigi + rose)
dish
double punch
egg & the urban mercantile
erica tanov
fantastico
fiddlesticks
flora grubb gardens
gamescape
goorin hat shop
harputs market
herringbone
hida tool
in fiore
kamei retaurant supply
kayo books
lavish
lemon twist
little otsu (online only)
lola (online only)
march
metier
mollusk surf shop
monument
my trick pony
nancy boy
nida
park life
paxton gate
peace industry
propeller
self edge
super7

supple
tail of the yak
tal-y-tara tea & polo shoppe
the ark
the ribbonerie
the wok shop
thomas e. cara
twelve sense media
(now mado creative)
velvet da vinci
william stout books
x21
yone of sf
zoe bikini

pacific heights

lower pacific heights, cow hollow,
japantown, western addition

benkyodo

japanese confectionary

1747 Buchanan Street
At Sutter (Japantown) *map E01*
415.922.4244
www.benkyodocompany.com

mon - sat 8a - 5p
breakfast. lunch. treats
$ cash only
first come, first served

Yes. Please: *manju: dorayaki, fukashi, chofu, kuri goma, kinako, pink habutai; fountain counter*

I'm constantly searching for places that feel like they are part of a bygone era. At **Benkyodo**, what caught my attention was the '70s style fountain counter. I could imagine coming in here during that era in my white San Francisco Riding Gear jeans to have a tuna melt and a Fresca. But the real story of **Benkyodo** is the mochi and manju that are made on site. Suyeichi Okamura began making these Japanese confections in 1906. Now over 100 years later, his grandsons are running the show. This is a great example of bygone not being gone at all, but better than ever.

bun mee

uptown banh mi

2015 Fillmore Street
Corner of Pine
(Lower Pacific Heights) *map E02*
415.800.7696
www.bunmee.co

sun – thu 10:30a - 9p
fri – sat 10:30a - 9:30p
lunch. dinner
$ first come, first served

Yes. Please: *mama tran's crispy egg rolls, mango sesame salad, hanoi style crispy catfish sandwich, mekong shrimp salad, caramel citrus rice bowl, coconut cookie sandwich*

In searching for really delicious banh mi sandwiches, my first inclination is to go to tiny, grimy joints. You know, the type of places that have one chair, a couple of laminated plastic menus with color photos and a scurrying floor pest that you try to ignore seeing. **Bun Mee** is the antithesis of this type of place. Yes, it's small—being in here when it's busy is like jamming 30 people into a Fiat 500—but it's a welcoming, groovily designed spot that buzzes with happy eaters. Denise Tran has fun with her menu and adds lots of twists to Vietnamese standards. And if you were thinking of leaving without a coconut cookie sandwich, you best think again—it's divine.

clary sage organics

organics to wear and to revive

2241 Fillmore Street
Corner of Clay (Pacific Heights) *map S01*
415.673.7300
www.clarysageorganics.com

twitter @clarysageorg
mon - sat 10a - 7p
sun 11a - 6p
online shopping. wellness center

Yes, Please: *clary sage: yoga wear, wellness solutions; stewart+brown, nau, linda loudermilk, prairie underground, farmaesthetics, intelligent nutrients, benedetta*

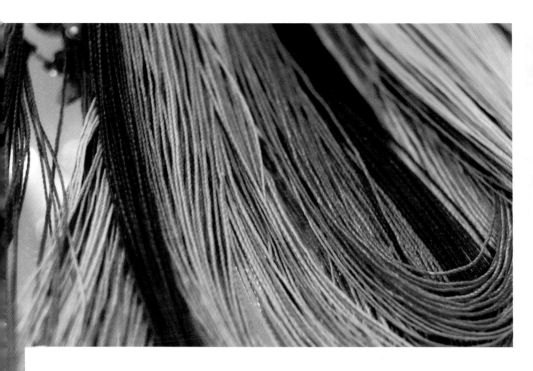

Here's the thing I find the hardest about being part of a small business that requires 192% of my time: things fall apart. Specifically, my body. There's always an ache or a sniffle or something that's messing with the mechanics. But **Clary Sage Organics** makes me feel there's hope on the horizon. First I would sign up with a wellness coach and take full advantage of some—okay, I might need all—of their wellness solutions, like the deep defense tea. And yoga would go on the docket, so some pieces from the **Clary Sage** yoga collection would be key. I feel better already.

conifer

fresh & easy clothing

2848 Webster Street
Corner of Union (Cow Hollow) *map S02*
415.922.1892
www.conifershop.com

mon - sat 11a - 7p sun noon - 5p
online shopping

Yes, Please: *pendleton "portland" line, current/elliott, dace, uzi, rachel comey, lauren moffat, swedish hasbeens, ace & jig, aesa, lacoli & mccallister, blithe + bonny candles*

I just looked at my tagline for this lovely little boutique and realized it reads a bit like a clothing detergent ditty. Even if my tagline is a bit blithe, **Conifer** is to be taken seriously. The clothing that owner Amy Mautz picks for her store is exactly what I, and many other women, want to wear—it's modern, yet easy and yes, it's fresh. And ladies, don't be too narcissistic while here, because there's plenty o' things for the men in your life, including big cozy sweaters that are meant to be borrowed. Gosh, I'm back to the self-centered thing...

ichiban kan

practical japanese items

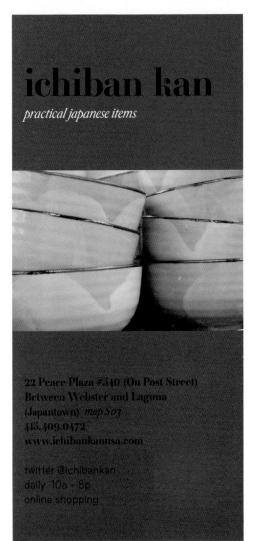

22 Peace Plaza #540 (On Post Street)
Between Webster and Laguna
(Japantown) *map S03*
415.409.0472
www.ichibankannusa.com

twitter @ichibankan
daily 10a – 8p
online shopping

Yes, Please: *smile mini sauce bottles, country kitchen gingham bento boxes, apple chan lip cream, slimity roller for body, baby foot deodorant spray*

Ichiban Kan is a danger to my bank account. Leave me alone in here for 30 minutes with an unlimited budget to spend and I will go bonkers. Oh wait, I did go bonkers in here for 30 minutes at my last visit, and I'm not broke. The brilliance of **Ichiban Kan** is you don't need an unlimited budget—think of it as an Asian dollar store. You'll find folks crowding the aisles here for everything from ramen and panko breading to cola-scented erasers and rice ball makers. I'm itching to go as I'm just writing this. I've got the **Ichiban Kan** fever.

jak home

a vision for modern living

2423 Polk Street
Between Filbert and Union
(Russian Hill) *map S04*
415.931.3868
www.jak-home.com

twitter @jakhome
tue - fri 1 - 6p
sat - sun 11a - 5p
design services

Yes, Please: *reagan bayes furniture, oly studio stools, robert true vice lamp, juliska glass, arteriors sabine table lamp, dransfield & ross driftwood side table*

Over the holidays I spent a lot of time in other people's houses throwing parties. Though I've never felt anything but love for my house, after spending time in these gorgeously decorated abodes, I got a big whopping complex. I was shocked into the realization that my house décor was still firmly planted in "just getting a grip that I'm an adult and have randomly decorated my house" style. Oi. I need owners Jeff and Kathleen's help. If their little Russian Hill showcase **Jak Home** (which fronts **Navarra Design Studio**) was transferred into my house, I guarantee my complex would disappear. Just like that.

nest

an exciting retail journey

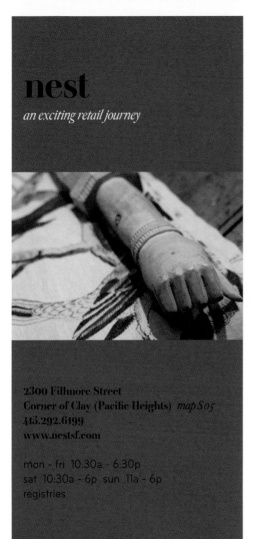

2300 Fillmore Street
Corner of Clay (Pacific Heights) *map S05*
415.292.6199
www.nestsf.com

mon - fri 10:30a - 6:30p
sat 10:30a - 6p sun 11a - 6p
registries

Yes, Please: *chiratorn dhira pravati vases, oleana blankets & beanies, patch scarves, let me be dress, lisa corti bedding, danielle wellman jewelry*

I can't lie. I am nuts about **Nest**, which is why it was featured in all of the *eat.shop san francisco* editions and now this new edition of *rather*. I'm sure some would say this reeks of favoritism, and they would be absolutely right. But I couldn't tell as compelling an SF shopping story if this legendary boutique was left out. Therefore it's in. Again. And what makes **Nest** so damn special that I'm willing to go out on this limb? When you enter here, you are transported beyond this city. One moment you're in India, next Sweden, then China. It's like having a round-the-world airline ticket all at one address.

spqr
the flavors of italy

1911 Fillmore Street
Between Pine and Bush
(Pacific Heights) *map E03*
415.771.7779
www.spqrsf.com

twitter @ spqrfillmore
dinner mon - sat 5:30 - 10:30p
sun 5:30 - 10p
brunch sat - sun 11a - 2:30p
$$-$$$ reservations recommended

Yes, Please: *08 elena walch, gewürztraminer, alto adige; fritto misto of local sole & fall vegetables, eggs al diavolo; duck ravioli, docetto sour cherries & sage*

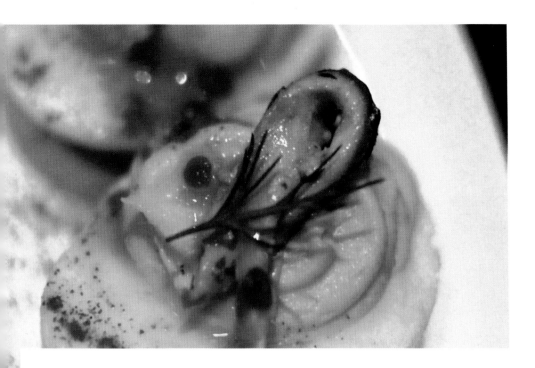

When a restaurant first opens, there are a whole lotta obstacles. The hope is that good press will come and with that, a full house. But what happens when the honeymoon ends and/or some of the original team move on? This is what happened at **SPQR**. When it opened in '07, the buzz was deafening, as this was the same team behind the beloved **A16**. But after the initial glow, Chef Nate Appleman left for the Big Apple. Shelley Lindgren, co-owner and sommelier extraordinaire, then showed her mettle by bringing in the talented Matt Accarrino to helm the kitchen, and the second coming of **SPQR** blossomed. Some argue it tops **SPQR** v.1. Whatever. It's just plain good.

the brooklyn circus

a unique urban style for men

1521 Fillmore Street
Near Geary (Western Addition) *map S06*
415.359.1999
www.thebkcircus.com

twitter @thebkcircussf
tue – sat noon – 7p
sun noon – 6p
online shopping

Yes, Please: *the brooklyn circus: varsity jackets, gatsby cap, reversible bow ties, velour cardigans, denim duffle; sebago boots, happy socks*

As much as I love a guy who can wear a pair of Levi's and a white t-shirt with unaffected panache, I also love a man who can peacock a bit, but not in a Vegas, silk-screened collared, striped shirt untucked sort of way. I'm talking **The Brooklyn Circus** style. While I was shooting here, I was chit-chatting with two of the **BKC** guys and was struck by how they wore their togs, mixing vibrant colors with patterns in a super fresh, urban updated *Cooleyhighharmony* type of way. There's a tribe of **BKC** types out there, growing steadily nationwide, and panache is their middle name.

timeless
treasures

a comely little haven of good things

2176 Sutter Street
Between Steiner and Pierce
(Lower Pacific Heights) *map S07*
415.775.8366
www.timelesstreasuressf.com

mon - sat 11a - 6p
sun 1 - 5p

Yes. Please: *viva vivande wooden cutting board,*
vintage letters and lots of 'em!, studiopatró tea towels,
vintage musical instrument rubber stamps

I love my job, and luckily I do, because complaining about eating and shopping for a living would put me into the whiners' hall of fame. And when I meet someone who is as enthusiastic about what they do as storeowner Joan O'Connor, I just want to sit down and shoot the breeze. From the moment we started talking, I knew we were like-minded types, as she loves nothing better than exploring a city, sniffing about all of the nooks and crannies. And when you visit her charming retreat of both vintage goods and new, **Timeless Treasures**, you'll be the beneficiary of her hunting skills.

hayes valley

lower market, upper haight

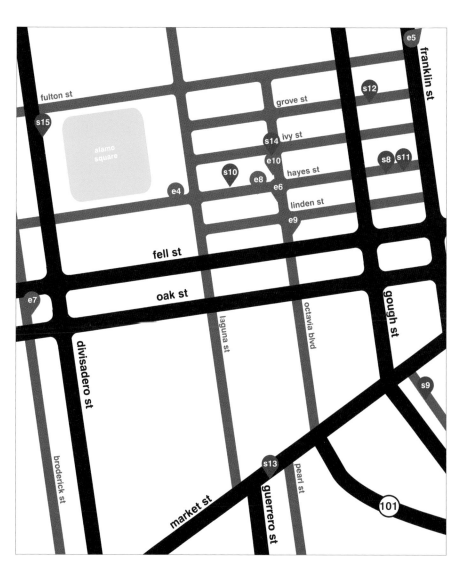

acrimony

a stylish reality

333 Hayes Street #102
Between Franklin and Gough
(Hayes Valley) *map So8*
see website for second location
415.861.1025
www.shopacrimony.com

twitter @shopacrimony
mon - sat 11a - 7p
sun noon - 6p
online shopping

Yes, Please: *kaylee tankus, acne, april 77, funktional, rad hourani, wings & horns, gitman brothers, nom de guerre*

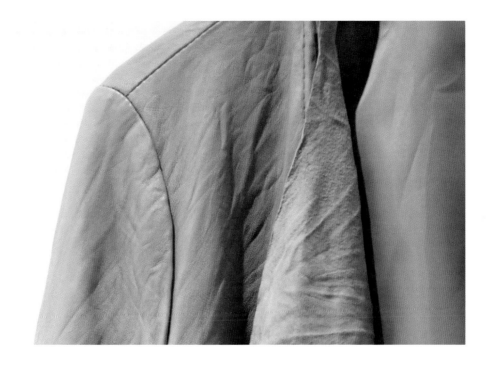

When I think about the word acrimony, I can't help but take the leap to the word acrimonious, and then all I can think about is bad reality television like Jon and Kate and any number of not-so-real housewives. When I think about the shop named **Acrimony**, all images of sniveling, warring tv numbskulls are banished, and I think of tasteful women's and men's clothing that is both stylish and trend-driven, but not mindlessly trendy. Do I think Snooki might buy something from here? Pleasssse. Would I? In a reality show second. And I'm looking forward to shopping at their brand new North Beach store Acre/SF.

bar jules

charming little neighborhood bistro

609 Hayes Street
Corner of Laguna (Hayes Valley) *map E.04*
415.621.5482
www.barjules.com

twitter @barjulessf
lunch wed - sat 11:30a - 2:30p
dinner tue - sat 6 - 10p
brunch sun 11a - 2:30p
$$ first come, first served

Yes, Please: *la bête pinot noir, fresh mint tisane, chickpea soup with cumin, house-cured sardines with new potato salad, wood-grilled skirt steak*

When I arrived at Bar Jules to take pictures, the doors had yet to open for the night. So I plopped myself down at an outside chair. Then a man showed up. He looked at the door. He looked at me. And then he stood right in front of the door, intent on being the first person to enter **Bar Jules**. I understood his determination. Owner and chef Jessica Boncutter has created a perfect little bistro where the food is spot on and the atmosphere cozy, with the perfect amount of buzz. By the time I left, the man was tucking into his main course, a look of contentment on his face.

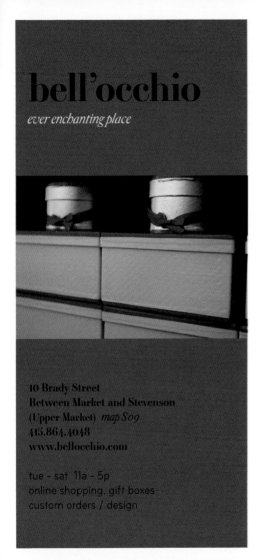

bell'occhio

ever enchanting place

10 Brady Street
Between Market and Stevenson
(Upper Market) *map S09*
415.864.4048
www.bellocchio.com

tue - sat 11a - 5p
online shopping. gift boxes
custom orders / design

Yes, Please: *handmade french boxes, l'ecritoire writing set, antique french rock crystal ring, marie antoinette & menagerie, bell'occhio cake stands*

I have an alternate universe that exists in my dreams. The Paris of my sleeping hours is vastly different from the real City of Light, so much so that when I visit the city, I'm always looking for the streets in my dreams. Recently I dreamt about **Bell'occhio**, but it was identical to the real one. I'm guessing my subconscious didn't play its usual trick because this place is a dream to behold. Owner Claudia Schwartz is a brilliant retail storyteller, and she methodically sources artisan crafted objects that range from ribbons to German chalf to French chapeux. **Bell'occhio** falls firmly into the category of "not to be missed."

birch

*where flowers and printed
matter converge*

564 Hayes Street
Between Laguna and Octavia (Hayes Valley)
3263 Sacramento Street *map S10*
Corner of Presidio (Pacific Heights)
hv: 415.626.6860 / ph: 415.922.4724
www.birchsf.com

twitter @birchsf
see website for hours
custom design / orders
deliveries. installations

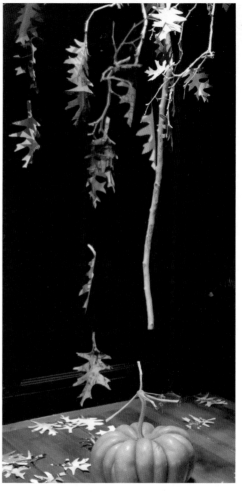

Yes, Please: *flowers, flowers, flowers; in fiore
parfum solide, william eggleston "2 1/4," cocoa absolute,
well curated selection of magazines, egg press cards*

My first magazine memory was reading Sunset in the '70s. By the time I was in high school, I was addicted to *W.* Then came college and I headed to NYC for design school so I could study to become a magazine art director. My obsession peaked during those years and I still have the piles of vintage mags to show for it. So the perfectly curated magazine wall at **Birch** in Hayes Valley is all that and more for me. I should amend that and say that the "more" refers to the glorious flowers—owner Torryne is a wizard with the stems. I'll need one arm to carry the mags and the other to carry a glorious, big bouquet.

lers ros

non-americanized thai

730 Larkin Street
Between O'Farrell and Ellis
(Tendernob) *map E05*
415.931.6917
www.lersros.com

daily 11a - midnight
lunch. dinner
$-$$ first come, first served

Yes, Please: *chrysanthemum drink, chang beer, look chin phing, yum koh moo yang, poh-tak, khao na phed, pad ped nok, yum pak karrd dong*

For the food obsessed, it's important to define and search out places that are authentic—in other words, places that have not been overly sullied by the American palate. One cuisine that foodies desire a pure experience with is Thai, and they are often disappointed in their quest. That was until **Lers Ros** opened. Here's a menu that has items like duck larb, house special frog and garlic and pepper rabbit. Can you imagine the joy of the San Francisco fooderati when they discovered chef Tom Silargorn's cooking? I'm amazed there wasn't a ticker tape parade down Van Ness.

lotus bleu

colorful home décor

325 Hayes Street
At Franklin (Hayes Valley) *map S11*
415.861.2700
www.lotusbleudesign.com

mon - fri 11a - 6p sat 11a - 7p
sun noon - 5p
online ordering. custom orders / design.
design services

Yes, Please: *custom order: settee, danish rocker, pillows; muskhane wool felt rugs, madeline weinrib tibetan carpets, john robshaw bedding*

Spring has finally arrived and I'm looking outside my window at rows of bright yellow, purple, red and orange tulips. And I'm immediately transported back to **Lotus Bleu**. Walking in here feels like a tulip field translated into furniture and rugs and bedding and home accessories. If your inclination is to live in a house swathed in stainless steel and tones of greige, then **Lotus Bleu** might make you rethink your decorating style, as it's so seductively happy to be surrounded by all this color. And just about everything you see is customizable and made-to-order. Color me pretty.

mac

modern appealing clothing for men and women

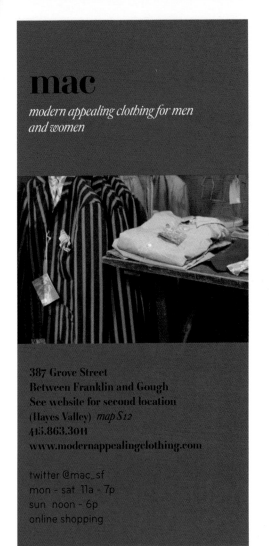

387 Grove Street
Between Franklin and Gough
See website for second location
(Hayes Valley) *map S12*
415.863.3011
www.modernappealingclothing.com

twitter @mac_sf
mon - sat 11a - 7p
sun noon - 6p
online shopping

Yes, Please: *yoshi kondo, dries van noten, sofie d'hoore, dema, walter van beirendonck, engineered garments, j.w. brine, sunny sports, lemon twist*

Here's a little history of 1980: Mount St. Helens blew, spewing ash to the moon and back, Bjorn Borg beat John McEnroe to win Wimbledon, John Lennon left this world, and **Modern Appealing Clothing** came to be. Though most of these people or things are now footnotes of history, **MAC** is still around, fresher and more cutting-edge than ever (with a brand new store in the Dogpatch neighborhood). I always look forward to visiting this place to see owners Chris and Ben's discoveries, and though they champion established designers like Dries Van Noten, they are always pushing the envelope and introducing new talents. **MAC**, now and forever, makes fashion fun.

miette
pâtisserie &
confiserie

my favorite place

449 Octavia Street
Between Linden and Hayes
(Hayes Valley) *map E06*
1 Ferry Building, #10 End of Market
(Embarcadero)
hv: 415.626.6221 / e: 415.837.0300
www.miette.com

twitter @miettecakes
see website for hours
treats
$-$$ first come, first served

Yes, Please: *chocolate tomboy cake, mini scharffen berger cakes, rose geranium parisian macaron, banana cream tart, lemon verbena cotton candy, mast brothers chocolate*

It was a bitter day when I learned late last year that Miette Confiserie off of Hayes was going to close. I bought a bag of goodies and took a long look at my dream candy store one last time. One tear escaped. Okay, that's not true. But what is true is when I revisited this area last March, I walked past **Miette** to mourn a bit, and jeepers!, it was open. Then I almost did cry. This is one of the prettiest spots to ever grace the pages of these books and Meg's baked goods are dee-vine. And did I tell you they are making cotton candy to order? Thank you sugar gods for answering my prayers.

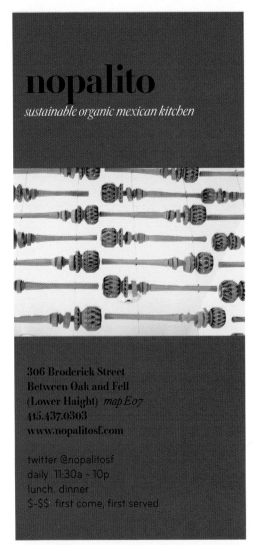

nopalito

sustainable organic mexican kitchen

306 Broderick Street
Between Oak and Fell
(Lower Haight) *map E07*
415.437.0303
www.nopalitosf.com

twitter @nopalitosf
daily 11:30a - 10p
lunch. dinner
$-$$ first come, first served

Yes, Please: *hibiscus valencia orange sparkling drink, chile chocolate milk, panucho de pollo al pibil, tamal en pipianodo de puerco*

There are many corners of this city that are food destinations, but the intersection of Broderick and Oak covers a number of bases. First head for **Nopalito**, which was inspired by the staff meals that chefs Gonzalo and Jose cooked at **Nopa**. The owners of **Nopa** recognized the simple brilliance of the duo's Mexican dishes and **Nopalito** came to be—SF has gone mad for this place. After cleaning your plate (like I did), if you realize your fridge is empty, go next door to **Falletti** Foods / Delessio Market & Bakery to stock up. It's a one-stop dining and shopping experience.

rare device

lotsa good stuff

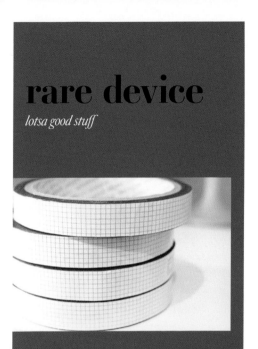

1845 Market Street
Between Guerrero and Pearl
(Upper Market) *map S13*
415.863.3969
www.raredevice.net

twitter @raredevice
tue - sat noon - 7p
sun noon - 6p
online shopping

Yes, Please: *kimura glass droplet, prismera jewelry, portland general store men's fragrances, roost floating feather ornaments, sagaform mortar & pestle*

Twitter is a seductive virtual beast. I tried to keep away from it for a while, but then it sucked me in like a tornado and I started fishing around for people or places that had something interesting to say or to show. At some point Lisa Congdon, an SF illustrator, popped up and her tweets fulfilled both my criteria, so I followed. Then I realized (duh) that Lisa was one of the owners of **Rare Device** with Rena Tom of the original outpost in NYC. Suddenly Twitter seemed useful, just as **Rare Device** is if you like smart, well-curated design shops as much as I do.

reliquary

beautiful goods contained here

**1537 Octavia Street
Between Grove and Hayes
(Hayes Valley)** *map S14*
**415.431.4000
www.reliquarysf.com**

tue - sat 11a - 7p sun noon - 6p

Yes, Please: *reliquary house line, arnsdorf, court jeans, 19 4t, jas m.b. bags, incense of the west, maasai beaded bracelets, mariska haskell jewelry*

Never one to shy away from morbid objects, I've always been fascinated with the concept of reliquaries. Over the years I've peered into many an ancient, ornate container, intrigued by the remains that lie within and the story of the life that once was. I was just as fascinated by **Reliquary**, the store. Every glance tells a tale here—tribal jewelry sits next to modern canvas bags, jeans that will be worn well within urban boundaries pair up with a vintage-inspired tunics and dresses. It all adds up to a place where you'll find things that won't gather dust in your closet, but will become part of your personal history.

sebo

the fine art of sushi

517 Hayes Street
Near Octavia (Hayes Valley) *map E08*
415.864.2181
www.sebosf.com

twitter @sebosf
dinner tue - sat 6 - 10p
izakaya sun 6 - 11p
$$-$$$ first come, first served

Yes. Please: *orion beer, jinyu brave warrior sake, chef's selection sashimi, sakamushi (sake & butter steamed clams), nigiri: aoyagi (stimson clam), hirame (fluke)*

This is another one of those eating experiences that I could get gushy about, but I'm thinking I'll show some restraint. I really really really like **Sebo**—a lot. With that nugget of understatement on the table, I'll move on and explain. **Sebo** is the type of place that needs no hype nor hojive. It's all about the freshest and most interesting varieties of fish available. And when it gets into the capable hands of owner / chefs Michael Black and Danny Dunham, they honor it with a stellar and often simple preparation. If you are looking for beautiful sushi without the hyperbole, **Sebo** is up your eating alley.

smitten
ice cream

frozen goodness

432 Octavia Street #1A
Corner of Linden (Hayes Valley) *map E09*
415.863.1518
www.smittenicecream.com

twitter @smittenicecream
sun - thu noon - 9p fri - sat noon - 10p
treats
$ first come, first served

Yes, Please: *gravenstein apple with honey, sweet corn with blackberry sauce, tcho chocolate with candied jalapeno, olive oil with lavender shortbread, ice cream sandwich*

Because I'm married to a Kevin and I know a lot of Kevins, I feel like I have an affinity with an ice cream machine named Kelvin. My Kevin runs on a lot of hot air, but **Smitten's** Kelvin runs with liquid nitrogen that creates ice cream in a lickety quick 60 seconds. Ohhhh, Kelvin—you're so smooth and you do make the most scrumptious ice cream. On a steamy hot fall day I ingested the sweet corn with blackberry sauce delight in record time, which had me thinking I best come back and visit Kelvin again and again.

taste

the art of tea

555 Octavia Street
Between Grove and Ivy
(Hayes Valley) *map E10*
415.552.5668
www.tasteteasf.com

twitter @tasteteasf
daily 11a - 7p
tea. light meals. treats
$ first come, first served

Yes. Please: *tea: six melon seed, green snail spring, iron goddess; gong fu tea service, lotus bun, tea macaron, vietnamese sandwich*

Tea is many things: mysterious, elegant, complex. Which is why I feel guilty every time I gulp down a quick brew of some cheap green tea or an earl grey that's steeped for 8 seconds and has one note of flavor—bland. From the moment I stumbled into **Taste**, the owner Vincent had me at hello. Within minutes I was sitting and drinking full-bodied, fragrant tea with him, learning about the craft and ceremony of Chinese tea. This seductive atmosphere here entices you to slow down and take a moment out of your hectic day to just breathe and remember that life is better with a hot cup of tea in hand.

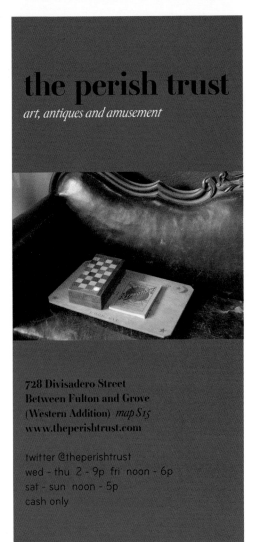

the perish trust

art, antiques and amusement

728 Divisadero Street
Between Fulton and Grove
(Western Addition) *map S15*
www.theperishtrust.com

twitter @theperishtrust
wed - thu 2 - 9p fri noon - 6p
sat - sun noon - 5p
cash only

Yes, Please: *mariele williams jewelry, andre nigoghossian glass, jessica niello paintings, kirsten finkas watercolors, kevin randolph lighting*

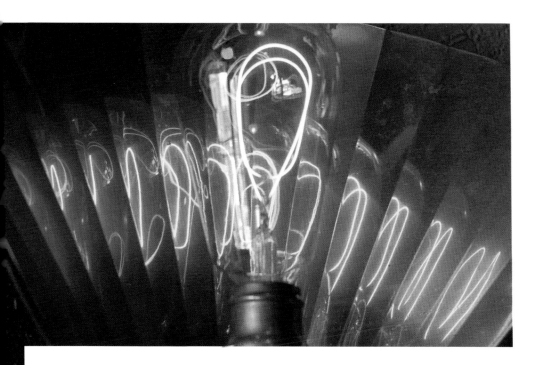

One of my favorite things to do as a kid was to go out to my grandparents' farm and spend hours rummaging through their 100-year-old barn. It was shadowy in there, so it was always a bit scary (was I worried about a ghost cow?), but once I got to digging through the years of stored antiques and whatnots, all worries disappeared. Poking through **The Perish Trust** brought back memories, though it doesn't smell like hay. Owners Kelly and Rod have collected an eclectic assortment of antiques and ephemera, and intermixed it with local artists' work. Sorry there's no ghost sheep, though.

north beach

jackson square, chinatown,
financial district, embarcadero

eat

shop

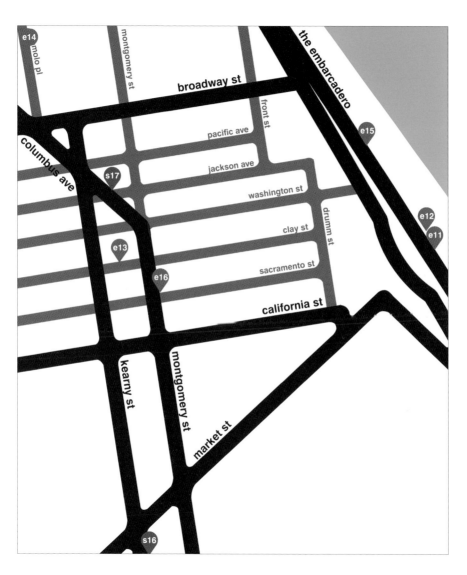

boccalone

tasty salted pig parts

1 Ferry Building, #21
End of Market Street
(Embarcadero) *map E11*
415.433.6500
www.boccalone.com

twitter @boccalone
mon - fri 9:30a - 6p
sat 8a - 6p sun 11a - 5p
lunch. dinner
$-$$ online shopping.
first come, first served

Yes, Please: *salumi cones, muffaletta sandwich, la cic-ciolina sandwich, easton's breakfast sausage, salumi: lardo, brown sugar & fennel, nduja*

I am a designer, and with that comes a ridiculous obsession with packaging. The first time I visited **Boccalone**— the purveyor of artisanal salumi—I loved the packaging, but because it was so well done and sharp, I worried that the product might be secondary to the outer casing. Wrong, wrong, wrong on my part, and I was told so by most of the food community in SF. Owner and chef Chris Cosentino is no poseur (as those who have eaten at his other venture, **Incanto**, know). He's curing meats the right way: small batch production using darn good pigs, which as the tagline states, makes tasty, salted pig parts. Yes indeedy.

cask

artisanal beverage purveyors

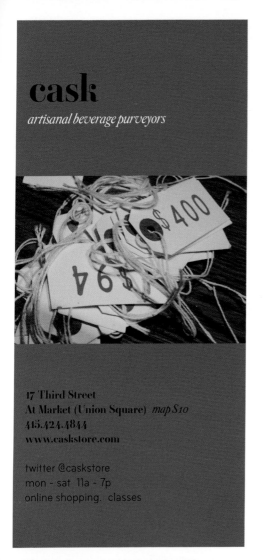

17 Third Street
At Market (Union Square) *map S10*
415.424.4844
www.caskstore.com

twitter @caskstore
mon - sat 11a - 7p
online shopping. classes

Yes. Please: *tequila querida viejo, connemara peated single malt whiskey, ransom old tom gin, toro albala viejisimo solera sherry, scrappy's grapefruit bitters*

Though I like an icy cold beer while eating spicy food and I am contractually obligated to drink wine because my husband sells it for a living, what I really like is liquor. Though I could bandy about the "liquor is quicker" cliché, I think that sounds a bit daft coming out of anybody's mouth over the age of 25. So I'll just say that **Cask** is a great bottle shop with a vast selection of hooch, much of it being of the hard-to-find variety and artisanally crafted. Along with the alcoholic goods are tools of the cocktail trade, which can come in handy when slinging your own drinks.

eden & eden

whimsical design boutique

560 Jackson Street
Corner of Columbus (North Beach) *map S17*
415.983.0490
www.edenandeden.com

mon – fri 10a – 7p
sat 10a – 6p
online shopping

Yes, Please: *cheeky mice, tatty devine pins & necklaces, vintage enamel necklaces, bus roll - 140 harrow, ivana helsinki anything, donna wilson fox cushion*

Though I love my brother, I don't think I could run a business with him. This sibling thing doesn't seem to be a problem, though, for Rachel and her brother Chas. Their labor of brotherly and sisterly love is the always wonderful, always whimsical design boutique **Eden & Eden**. Every time I visit here it's a guarantee that something (or many things) will make me smile. This visit I was tickled by the John and Yoko mice. I'm still cracking up thinking of them. Seriously, though, I never leave without making a purchase. It's impossible to do so. I dare you to try.

il cane rosso

casual rotisserie

1 Ferry Building, #41
End of Market Street
(Embarcadero) *map E12*
415.391.7599
www.canerossosf.com

twitter @canerossosf
see website for hours
breakfast. lunch. dinner
$-$$ first come, first served

Yes, Please: *fentiman dandelion-burdock soda, scrimshaw pilsner, spit-roasted porchetta, marin sun farms beef stracotto, roasted carrots & parsnips*

I'm slightly embarrassed to admit that of all the tempting items (and there are quite a few) on Il Cane Rosso's menu, the first thing that caught my attention was the Straus Dairy vanilla soft serve. Though I'm thinking a visit to a food shrink would be helpful to figure out this attraction, I came to my senses quickly and ordered the porchetta. Oh holy pig, it was good. Il Cane Rosso is inspired by the small sandwich shops and rotisseries of Southern Italy, which is in American terms something akin to a place that serves slow food (i.e., food carefully and lovingly prepared) in a flash. I'll give up soft serve any day to eat this type of fare.

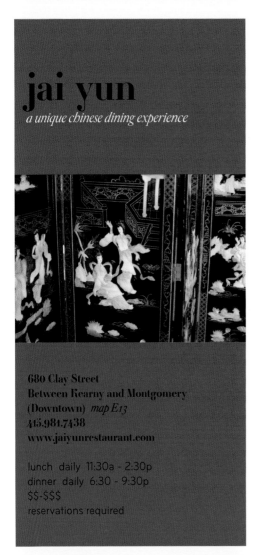

jai yun

a unique chinese dining experience

680 Clay Street
Between Kearny and Montgomery
(Downtown) *map E13*
415.981.7438
www.jaiyunrestaurant.com

lunch daily 11:30a - 2:30p
dinner daily 6:30 - 9:30p
$$-$$$
reservations required

Yes, Please: *multiple course meal that could include: chinatown special cabbage, vegetarian goose, lotus root salad, poached chilled duck*

Though dozens of restaurants in SF's Chinatown are happy as all get to serve kung pao chicken to the tourist trade, it's not so easy to find a place to have a meal that truly excites the senses. Then there's **Jai Yun**. Here's how it's supposed to work: Call and make a reservation so Chef Nei' knows how many he's cooking for at that meal. Once you're seated, a member of the wait staff who doesn't speak much English will ask what price of meal you want. Be forewarned, it can get spendy—$80 and upward per person depending on the complexity. Once the price is defined, sit back and wait for the magic. Multiple small courses will appear, each more delicious than the last. Though your wallet will be somewhat lighter, your food soul will be happy.

little vine

sweet little neighborhood market

1541 Grant Avenue
Between Filbert and Union
(North Beach) *map E14*
415.738.2221
www.shoplittlevine.com

tue - fri 11a - 7p sat 10a - 7p sun 10a - 5p
grocery
$-$$ first come, first served

Yes. Please: *bicycle coffee, bundaberg australian ginger beer, housemade sandwiches, achadinha "capricious" goat cheese (rubbed with lard), heslet honey co. honey*

I don't think of myself as a backwardist. What I mean is that I don't desire to live in a past era, but at one point as a kid I did wish I was Laura Ingalls Wilder living on a farm, but I've gotten over that. I do wish though there were more corner markets in this modern age. A perfect example of this is **Little Vine**. Oh how I would love to live in North Beach. I'd be dropping by this food nook to chat with owners Melissa and Jay while sipping a coffee, grabbing a bottle of wine and some cheese for later in the day. I might pop in later to get the olive oil I forgot I was out of. This is what you do when you're lucky enough have a neighborhood market like **Little Vine**.

tcho

chocolate as a cure-all

Pier 17
At Green (Embarcadero) *map E15*
415.981.0189
www.tcho.com

twitter @ tchochocolate
mon - fri 9a - 5p sat - sun 10a - 5p
treats
$ first come, first served

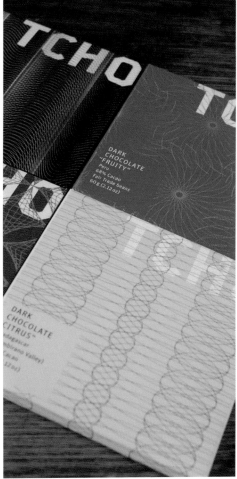

Yes, Please: *tcho chocolate: hot chocolate,
organic baking drops, tcho-a-day: 30 / 60 / 90 supply,
chocolate-drenched mango, roasted nibs*

DARK CHOCOLATE
"CITRUS"

Some people eat an apple a day, some people pop vitamins each morning for vigor, but my health regimen requires a **Tcho**-a-day. Though this prescription might seem a wee bit out of the ordinary, I highly recommend it. What could be better for the body than a good dose of dark chocolate? If you read **Tcho's** website you'll see it uses big words like Theobromine and Phenethylamine to talk about the health benefits. If you want the quick translation, these words mean "quit reading and eat the chocolate, dummy." Which is what I did, and I'm aglow. I'm a **Tcho** believer.

wexler's

modern bbq

568 Sacramento Street
Corner of Montgomery
(Financial District) *map E16*
415.983.0102
www.wexlerssf.com

see website for hours
lunch. dinner
$$ reservations recommended

Yes. Please: *north coast brewing prangster ale, basil haydens scotch, zuckerman farm shaved asparagus salad, bbq california quail, smoked short rib*

I know that I've already blah-blah'd about this, but I can get pretty wrapped up in the packaging of things, and if the outer wrapping seems a bit too slick, I become suspicious. So you would think my radar would be up in accordance to **Wexler's**, where the food is Southern barbeque inspired, but the décor is urban cool with a massive ceiling installation that looks like a long, undulating black wave. But these details just add to the allure here, as does chef Charlie Kleinman's cooking, where he puts an uptown spin on some seriously down home food. Suspicions averted, I'm hooked.

soma

potrero hill, bernal heights

eat

shop

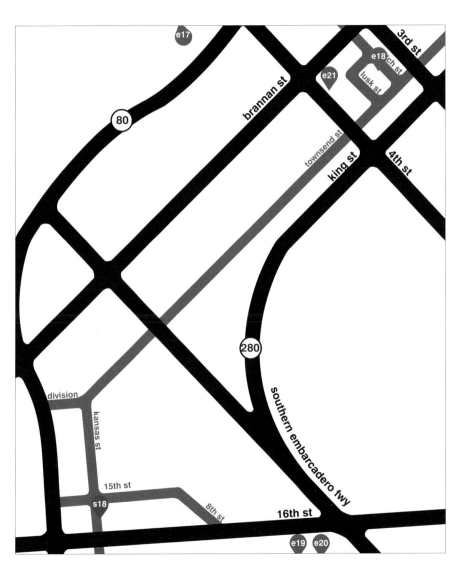

bar agricole

modern urban tavern

335 11th Street
Between Folsom and Harrison
(Soma) *map E17*
415.355.9400
www.baragricole.com

twitter @baragricole
see website for hours
brunch. dinner
$$ reservations recommended

Yes, Please: *manila hotel julep, bobby burns, roasted padrón, lipstick, corno di toro + jimmy nardello peppers with tonnato; sardine roll mops, chèvre + strawberry tart*

It seems like every book I've ever worked on, there's always been one restaurant that's gotten away. Bar Agricole was that place for this book, as it was scheduled to open right after the original production was complete. Drats. Thankfully, this update came about and **Bar Agricole** was numero uno on my restaurants to include. Sitting out on the front-loaded garden patio on a warm early fall evening taking pictures and sipping the drink shown at left confirmed what I had hoped. **Bar Agricole** was worth the wait.

battersea

industrial antiques and beyond

297 Kansas Street
Corner of 16th (Potrero Hill) *map S18*
415.553.8500
www.batterseasf.com

mon - fri 10a - 5p or by appointment
online shopping (1st dibs). design services

Yes, Please: *mounted caster table lamps, brutalist chandelier, leather studded side table, zinc industrial barrels, verdigris floodlight, dental cabinet*

One of these days I'm going to completely start over when it comes to the décor of my house, though starting over is kind of a joke since I never really got started. My husband and I seem to belong to the "sleep-decorating" school of philosophy when it comes to our home. If I could start over, I would choose a style that is modern but with a good dose of early-to-mid-20th century European and American industrialism thrown in. To find these pieces I would aim for **Battersea**, as owner Will Wick's collection is the cat's meow. I especially like how he repurposes objects like casters into lamps. Clever man, that Will.

little skillet

farm fresh soul food

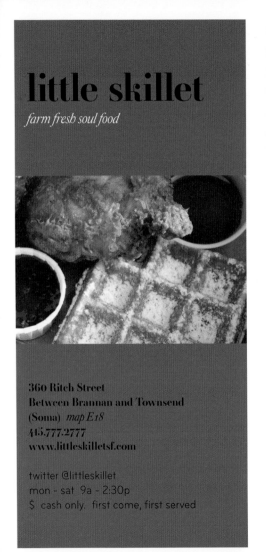

360 Ritch Street
Between Brannan and Townsend
(Soma) *map E18*
415.777.2777
www.littleskilletsf.com

twitter @littleskillet
mon - sat 9a - 2:30p
$ cash only. first come, first served

Yes. Please: *blue bottle coffee next door at centro, black-berry lemonade, egg mcmahon, chicken & waffles, grits with bacon, brown sugar & pecan*

When I'm working on these books, there are high points and low points. Though I could regale you with the lows (frat boy hot tubbers), I'd rather focus on the highs. Eating **Little Skillet's** fried chicken and waffles on a sunny spring morning while sitting on a loading dock in a SoMa alley was way high on the happy scale. Though this place is no more than a window attached to a kitchen the size of small dorm room, it puts out realllllly good Southern-style food. Which makes sense because the good folks of **Farmer Brown** are behind the venture.

plow

food worth moaning over

1299 18th Street
Corner of Texas
(Potrero Hill) *map E19*
415.821.7569
www.eatatplow.com

breakfast and lunch tue - fri 7a - 2p
brunch sat - sun 8a - 2p
$ - $$ first come, first served

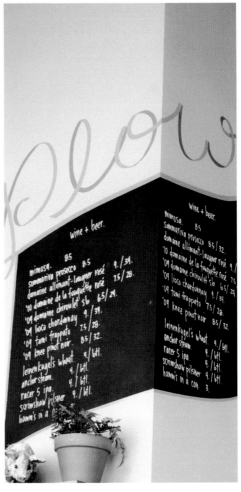

Yes, Please: *camellia blossoms iced tea, peach crostata, lemon ricotta pancakes, fried egg sandwich, chinese breakfast, late summer melon + mint salad, roast pork sandwich*

What is it about breakfast places and home fries? Does anyone like home fries? No, because they are at the bottom of the breakfast potato ladder. If you're looking for the top, look no further than the crunchy wonderland of the spuds at **Plow**. Can't you just taste how delectable these were? There was a woman at the table next to me with two friends who was rhapsodizing so passionately about the potatoes, I thought she was going to have a Meg Ryan *Sleepless in Seattle* moment, and I wouldn't have blamed her. Looking beyond this addictive starch, the other breakfast items here are equally as delicious, which is why this tiny place has a line of people waiting to get in. Take it from my moaning in pleasure neighbor–the wait is worth it.

sandbox
bakery

asian inspired bakery

833 Cortland Avenue
Corner of Gates (Bernal Heights) *map E20*
415.642.8580
www.sandboxbakerysf.com

twitter @sandboxbakery
mon - sat 6a - 3p sun 7a - 3p
$ first come, first served

Yes, Please: *chai / espresso hybrid, valrhona mocha, yuzu marmalade with sage pan, melon pan, chocolate banana hearts, sweet cheese croissant*

I'm sitting here playing a little word association game with myself. Cow = milk. Chocolate = eat lots of. Morning pastry = yuzu and sage. Say what? Okay, the only reason I made that leap was because of **Sandbox Bakery**. As I was standing in front of the case of baked delights here, some of them Asian inspired, I was drawn to the yuzu marmalade and sage pan. Okay, I was looking at about ten other things also, but this is what I went for, and I'm glad I did. Not too sweet, with the perfect hint of sagey herbalness—it rocked my early morning world.

sightglass
coffee bar &
roastery

sf's latest coffee sensation

270 Seventh Street
Between Folsom and Howard
(Soma) *map E21*
415.861.1313
www.sightglasscoffee.com

twitter @sightglass
mon - sat 7a - 7p sun 8a - 7p
coffee. treats
$ first come, first served

Yes, Please: *coffee roasts: blueboon blend, owl's howl espresso; macchiato, hooker's mocha, firebrand bakery chocolate brioche*

When I was in my mid 20s I had a verging on hallucinogenic experience with coffee. A friend had made me a cappuccino, and after slugging it down, my head began to spin. I felt like I was somewhere between Timothy Leary and Linda Blair in *The Exorcist.* Suffice to say, I've steered clear of the hard stuff since, but that doesn't stop me from being drawn in to a place like **Sightglass**. SF is a coffee crazy town where there's always a hot new coffee debutante on the scene, and these days that crown belongs to **Sightglass**. The cafe and roastery is a huge cathedral of a space where people line up like they are receiving the sacraments. God bless the bean.

outer sunset

inner richmond

eat

shop

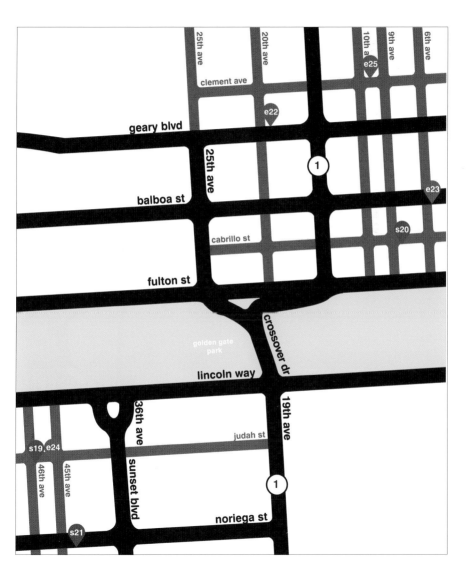

general store

*just what the name says, but with
a modern aesthetic*

4035 Judah Street
Between 45th and 46th (Outer Sunset) *map S19*
415.682.0600
www.visitgeneralstore.com

mon - fri 11a - 7p
sat - sun 10a - 7p
custom design / orders

Yes, Please: *jenny pennywood bags, hakusan porcelain,
vintage dairy site glass, manimal moccasins, "the printmaking bible" by ann d'arcy hughes*

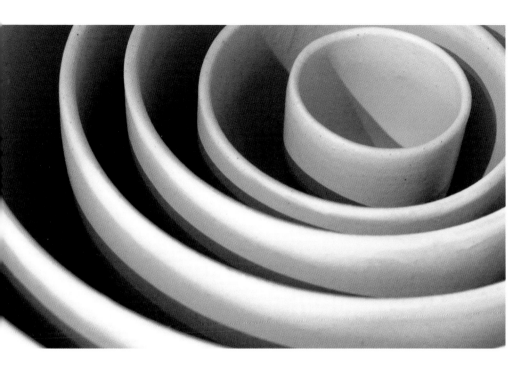

There's many a thing I like about this neck of the woods near Ocean Beach. As already noted, I like (love) Outerlands, and **Trouble Coffee** is pretty swell. I like the brine in the wind that's whipping off the ocean. And I like (with a couple of exclamation points) **General Store**. SF has a couple of really great, smartly-curated design shops, and this is certainly one of them. With its skatepark meets Santorini interior architecture and products that are just as eclectic, I would happily make the drive out here to take a gander.

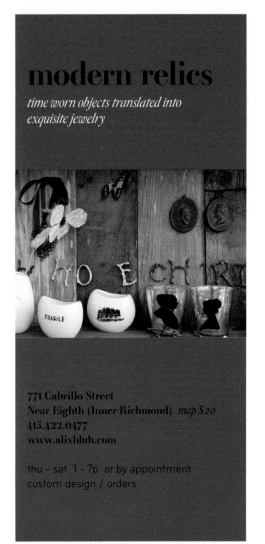

modern relics

time worn objects translated into exquisite jewelry

771 Cabrillo Street
Near Eighth (Inner Richmond) *map S20*
415.422.0477
www.alixbluh.com

thu - sat 1 - 7p or by appointment
custom design / orders

Yes, Please: *alix bluh: stag horn earrings, bramble bracelet, benevola necklace, eyeris necklace; diana fayt ceramics, swallow gilt paintings, suga jewelry*

When it comes to guides, I get a laugh when the term off-the-beaten-path is used. At the risk of sounding like a guide curmudgeon, almost all the *paths* in big cities are *beaten* pretty quickly, especially in this era of Twitter and blogs. So even though **Modern Relics** is tucked away on a quiet street, I'm not going to pretend I discovered it. I will, though, take ownership of how fantastic I think it is. Alix Bluh has transformed her jewelry workshop into an enchanted den that highlights the heirloomesque quality of her work and the complementary designs that tell the rest of the retail story. I'd beat a path here if I were you.

moscow & tbilisi bakery

great russian bakery

УРЕКИ, ХАЧА
ОЖКИ, СЛА
ЕНЬЯ, ПЕЛЬ
ОЧКИ С МА
МНОГОЕ ДР

5540 Geary Boulevard
Between 19th and 20th
(Inner Richmond) *map E22*
415.668.6959

daily 7a - 9p
$ cash only. first come, first served

Yes. Please: *chocolate potato log, halal breads, piroshki, borscht, khachapuri, walnuts in grape juice, blinses, poppy seed hamentashen*

Here is the perfect, kooky San Francisco snapshot. I pulled my car into a rare Inner Richmond weekend parking spot so I could go to the Russian bakery **Moscow & Tbilisi**. As I exited the car, a "Jingle Bells" serenade began coming from an elderly, toothless Asian man playing the accordian. Ahhh, yes—nothing like a continuous loop of annoying holiday jingles in March to put a grin on your face. What made me even more chipper was what was inside. Big, fat piroshkis and piles of brightly colored meringues and baked goods galore. Merry Christmas to me!!

namu

where californian cuisine meets up with the flavors of asia

439 Balboa Street
Between Fifth and Sixth
(Inner Richmond) *map E23*
415.386.8332
www.namusf.com

twitter @namusf
see website for hours
brunch, dinner
$$: first come, first served

Yes, Please: *thai chili soju infusion, sake flights, daily crudo with pickled battera konbu, shiitake dumplings in a dashi mushroom broth, lamb chops*

Fusion is a word that strikes fear in the hearts of many eaters, myself included. Whoever thought that marrying the flavors of the Caribbean with those of Italy should be locked up in the bad food idea jail. On occasion **Namu** has been called a fusion restaurant, but I would beg to differ. My take is that it's a place where the flavors of Korea, Japan and Thailand beautifully collide with the clean and healthy notes of Californian cuisine. This is super invigorating food that I could eat everyday. And though I am a card-carrying carnivore, **Namu's** menu is filled with vegetable dishes that put meat to shame.

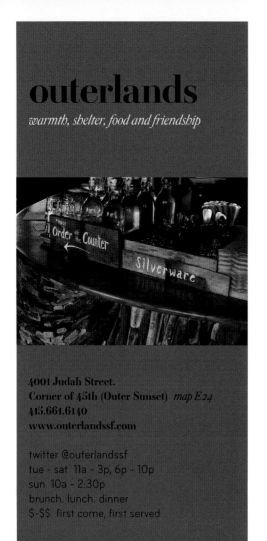

outerlands

warmth, shelter, food and friendship

4001 Judah Street.
Corner of 45th (Outer Sunset) *map E24*
415.661.6140
www.outerlandssf.com

twitter @outerlandssf
tue - sat 11a - 3p, 6p - 10p
sun 10a - 2:30p
brunch. lunch. dinner
$-$$ first come, first served

Yes, Please: *hot ginger lemon apple cider, chemex drip sightglass coffee, baked eggs with rosemary, eggs in jail, dutch pancake, goat cheese souffle*

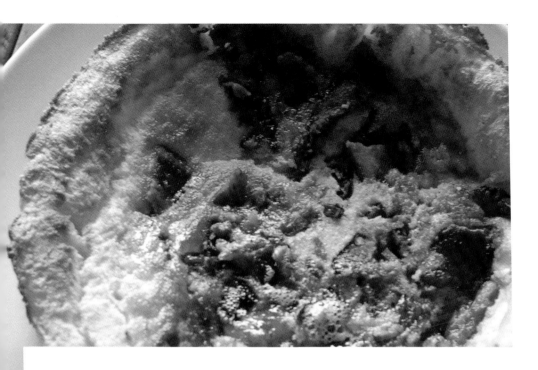

It's a Sunday morning, and I've got a Saturday night tv hangover. Though the sun is out, everything seems muted in my fuzzy world as I make the drive towards Outer Sunset. Everything changes, though, when I sit down in the wooden-planked **Outerlands**. The smells from Dave Muller's kitchen are ridiculous: brewing coffee mingling with the heavenly scents of fresh-baked bread and bacon frying. Suddenly the sun is bright and everything is in Technicolor. All I see are smiling people—even those waiting to get into this little beachside nirvana. Happiness is a meal at **Outerlands**.

singapore malaysian

the name of the restaurant says it all

836 Clement Street
Between Ninth and Tenth
(Inner Richmond) *map E25*
415.750.9518

mon, wed - thu 5 - 9:30p
sat - sun 11:30a - 9:30p
lunch, dinner
$ - $$ first come, first served

Yes, Please: *cendol, tiger beer, otak-otak, pou pia, ikan belendang, singaore chow bee hoon, hainan chicken & rice, bu bocha cha*

The hawker stalls of Singapore are some of my favorite places to eat on earth. I could do a long laundry list of beloved foods at these stalls, but I'll just name a few for the sake of time and your attention span: popiah, char kway teow, hainanese chicken and rice and fish head curry. Problem is, it's hard as heck to find this type of food—that's just as good—in the States. Hence why I swooned over **Singapore Malaysian**. No name fluffing here—just a straightforward moniker that lets you know the cuisine you will be devouring. Now I won't have to buy that zillion dollar ticket back to Singapore.

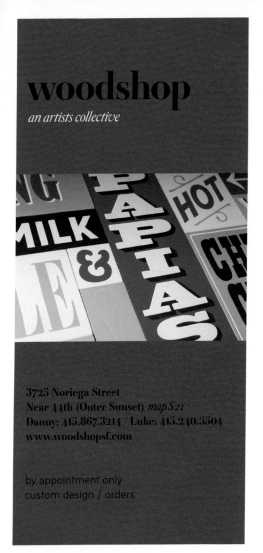

woodshop
an artists collective

3725 Noriega Street
Near 44th (Outer Sunset) *map S21*
Danny: 415.867.3214 / Luke: 415.240.5504
www.woodshopsf.com

by appointment only
custom design / orders

Yes, Please: *danny hess surfboards, luke bartels re/find furniture, jeff canham hand-painted sign & graphics, josh duthie's chairtastic*

Working on these books can be like doing a connect-the-dots puzzle. The first dot in SF was Danny Hess, whose custom-built, wood surfboards caught my eye. I was playing phone tag with him on the day I was shooting **Outerlands** and **General Store**. While in **GS**, I was lusting for a vintage chair and the owner Mason told me that Josh, the designer, had a studio a couple of blocks away with a guy building surfboards. Ding ding ding. I followed the dots to **Woodshop**, a big workspace that also houses Jeff, an amazing sign painter, and Luke, who handcrafts furniture from reclaimed wood. Dots connected.

mission

noe valley, castro

eat

shop

San Francisco

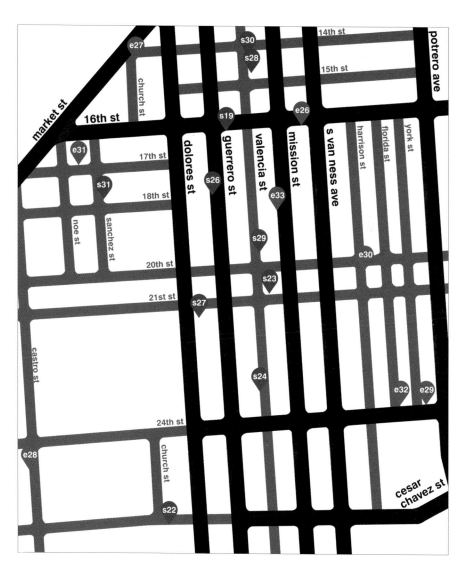

bar bambino

essential wine bar and café

2931 16th Street
Between Mission and Van Ness
(Mission) *map E26*
415.701.8466 (VINO)
www.barbambino.com

twitter @barbambino
mon - thu 5:30 - 10p
fri - sat 5p - midnight
$$ reservations accepted

Yes, Please: *selection of over 175 wines, house & artisanal cured meats, artisanal cheeses, olive oil flight, cestini stuffed with oxtail, puglian style lamb shank*

I find myself getting suspicious when somebody gushes about something. Are they being paid to be so positive? Is their discerning radar a bit skewed? Yet, here I am ready to gush about **Bar Bambino**. I really love this place. Love love love. And last I checked my offshore bank account, owner Christopher Losa is not paying me to say so. What's got me in such a lather? This is the type of spot that's fantastic because it comes without pretense and yet is carefully considered, from the thoughtful wine list to a cheese selection gorgeously displayed in its own glass room to the simple Italian cuisine. Love.

candystore collective

sweets in the form of clothing and gifts

3153 16th Street *map S22*
Between Guerrero and Valencia (Mission)
2226 Bush Street
Between Steiner and Fillmore
(Pacific Heights)
415.863.8143 / 888.601.0117
www.candystorecollective.com

twitter @candystorecolle
mon - sat noon - 7p
sun noon - 6p
online shopping

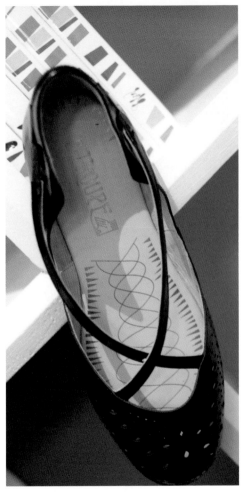

Yes, Please: *laeken dress, jene despain jewelry, yellow owl workshop cards, office wiederholt socks, fluffyco. tees, doily basket, the heated tea towels*

If I didn't make it crystal clear from my drooly love letter to Miette Confiserie, I've got a thing for candy. So if there's a store that's got candy somewhere in its name, there's a good chance that it will be in my good graces, like **Candystore Collective** is. Yes there's candy here, but that isn't what this beloved San Francisco boutique is all about. It is about a kickin' collection of spunky clothing and accessories for both guys and gals. Add a dash of groovy lifestyle items and you've got a recipe for good shopping. And they have a new store called **Hello by Candystore Collective** in the Fillmore District. Sweeeet.

chilango

wholesome mexican food

235 Church Street
At Market (Castro) *map E27*
415.552.5700
www.chilangorestaurantsf.com

daily 11a - 10p
$-$$ first come, first served

Yes, Please: *bohemia beer, guacamole chilango, cocktail de camaron, papas con huevo, duck flautas, huarache chilango, pambazo, chocolate mexicano*

If you live in or visit San Francisco, it is imperative to know a good place for a proper Mexican brunch. Nothing starts a day right or tempers a good old-fashioned hangover quite like huevos rancheros or migas or papas con huevos. Here's my suggestion: Go to **Chilango** and order any of the above mentioned dishes (I went for the papas). Get a side order of guacamole, which looks like it took five goliath avocados to make, take a big forkful of the guac and plop it on your eggs, then douse the dish with Cholula. Makes waking up before noon on the weekends worthwhile.

contigo
a food love letter to barcelona

1320 Castro Street
Corner of 24th (Noe Valley) *map E28*
415.285.0250
www.contigosf.com

twitter @contigosf
tue - sat 5:30 - 10p
sun 5:30 - 9:30p
$$ reservations recommended

Yes, Please: *isastegi sagardo naturala cider, jamón ibérico de bellota pata negra, calamars a la planxa with cara cara oranges, four course menu del dia, oxtail croquetas*

Some places, from the moment you walk in the door, have L-O-V-E written all over them. I don't mean in a romantic sort of way, I mean in a "the owners must really adore what they do" type of way. I felt this the moment I entered **Contigo**. Owners Elan and Brett were warm and welcoming, and families with pipsqueaks happily co-mingled with Gen Y types. I positioned myself at the bar so I could watch the cooks in action making their Spanish/Catalan dishes. And when some of those dishes came my way, here's what was written on my face: L-O-V-E.

dynamo
donut + coffee

modern donut outpost

2760 24th Street
Between York and Hampshire
(Mission) *map E29*
415.920.1978
www.dynamodonut.com

twitter @dynamodonut
tue - sat 7a - 5p sun 9a - 4p
$ cash only. first come, first served

glazed bacon apple

lemon thyme $2

sticky bun $3

mpkin chocolate chip

vanilla bean $2

coconut $2.50

ocolate star anise $

Yes, Please: *four barrel coffee, ginger lemonade,
donuts: maple glazed bacon apple, lemon thyme,
coconut, chocolate star anise, molasses pear guiness*

I think that Sara Spearin should have named her dee-lish-us donut spot Dy-no-mite so I could do my pathetic Jimmie Walker impression. Alas, she didn't ask me and named it **Dynamo Donut + Coffee**, which still gets the point across that these fried rounds of dough are outta this world. Even though I'm suspect of donut shops that make wacked out, stoneresque flavors like Nyquil glazed, I fully embrace Sara's creative recipes that taste amazing. The maple glazed bacon apple is hugely satisfying and should be considered a healthy meal, being that it covers four of the six food groups.

flour + water

neapolitan style pizza and fresh pasta

2401 Harrison Street
Corner of 20th (Mission) *map E30*
415.826.7000
www.flourandwater.com

twitter @flourandwater
sun – wed 5:30 – 11p
thu – sat 5:30p – midnight
$$ reservations accepted

Yes. Please: *08 weingut niklas sudtiroler lagrein,
yellowtail with radish & meyer lemon aioli,
pizza: biancoverde, salsiccia, topinambur*

In this era of scrimping and saving, there's been an explosion of spots serving simple, affordable foods: burgers, sandwiches and the ever popular pizza. SF and the East Bay are crawling with pizza joints, some of them appearing in the previous editions of the *eat.shop guides*: Pizzeria Delfina, Gialina, Piccino and Pizzaiolo, to name a few. So when it came time to work on this book, who would make the cut? In SF, **Flour + Water** is the pizza and pasta hot spot du jour. Whether you choose an inspired-by-the-motherland pie or a savory bowl of tajarin, or in my case, both, you can't go wrong.

frances

modern california cuisine

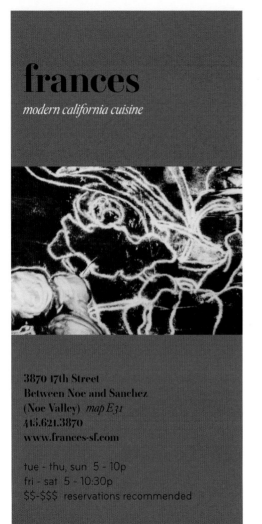

3870 17th Street
Between Noe and Sanchez
(Noe Valley) *map E31*
415.621.3870
www.frances-sf.com

tue - thu, sun 5 - 10p
fri - sat 5 - 10:30p
$$-$$$ reservations recommended

Yes, Please: *07 marco felluga pinot grigio, local dungeness crab salad, applewood smoked bacon beignets, bellwether farm ricotta gnocchi with green garlic*

As a child I remember that one of the lessons that was drilled into me was "Don't play favorites." And though I've got this lesson embedded in my mind, I'm ignoring it in **Frances's** case. I'm not going to be coy about how much I adore this place. What's so great about it? Let's start at the top. Melissa Perello makes delicious food that is pristine, but not pretentious. The staff is as good as they come: highly professional, but still über-friendly. The room is small and chic in an understated type of way, yet still cozy. Yes, I'm going to play favorites—I love **Frances**.

gravel & gold
beautiful bohemia

3266 21st Avenue
Corner of Lexington (Mission) *map S23*
415.552.0112
www.gravelandgold.com

twitter @gravelandgold
tue - sat noon - 7p sun noon - 5p
online shopping. classes.
customized services

Yes, Please: *peterboro ash bike baskets, unison tileworks, deadstock osborn & woods silkscreened cards, tripp carpenter wishbone chair*

Gravel & Gold is the modern equivalent to a coffee klatch sans the coffee. The day I was in here shooting and chatting, the three owners were animatedly ensconced in an ever-revolving social hive of interaction. Every person who came through the door was warmly greeted, whether friend or stranger, and soon became part of the conviviality. Each owner in turn became like a docent, talking about the provenance of each item, whether it be a piece of jewelry, a stripey t-shirt or a wall-hanging. I think **Gravel & Gold** is truly the bee's knees.

gypsy honeymoon

romantic antiques with a story to tell

1266 Valencia Street
Between 23rd and 24th (Mission) *map S24*
415.821.1713
www.gypsy-honeymoon.com

tue - sat 11a - 7p
sun 11a - 6p
cash only

Yes. Please: *guatemalan conquistador maps,*
albumen prints, alligator buttons, 1900's glass domes,
jes feuny talismans, french grave marker

Though I was tempted to use some of the lyrics from Kim Carnes' song "Gypsy Honeymoon" here, they are way too high on the schmaltz scale to co-opt. So I'll have to use my own words to talk about this beloved Mission antiques and curiosities shop. Though it's changed hands over the years and moved locations, the essence of **Gypsy Honeymoon** has stayed true to its ornate, romantic, a little macabre, Victoriana sensibilities. Owner Gabrielle Ekedal is a talented retail storyteller creating intriguing vignettes that leave the shopper pondering the tales behind these little snippets of days gone by.

la palma
mexicatessen

tortilleria y huaracheria

2884 24th Street
Corner of Florida (Mission) *map E32*
415.647.1500
www.lapalmasf.com

mon - sat 8a - 6p
sun 8a - 5p
$ first come, first served

Yes, Please: *handmade tortillas, nacatamales, papusas, tripas, masa, tacos de canasta, huarache, chicharron*

Though people usually go on and on about Mission-style burritos when they are talking about Mexican food in this city, I can get a whopper of a gas attack just thinking about those five pound bricks. What really rocks my boat is a good tortilla. You can watch them being made at **La Palma Mexicatessen** (I love this name), along with many other delights, like handmade masa, perfect for taking home and turning into tamales. There's something about this food that makes you feel like you have your very own Mexican grandmother lovingly making it for you.

mission chinese food

what's behind the doors at lung shan?

2234 Mission Street
Between 18th and 19th (Mission) *map E33*
415.863.5710
www.missionchinesefood.com

mon - tue, thu - sun 11:30a - 3p, 5 - 10:30p
lunch. dinner. delivery
$ - $$ first come, first served

Yes, Please: *cold dan dan noodles, tea-smoked eel, west-lake rice porridge, kung pao pastrami, sizzling cumin lamb, mongolian long beans, open-faced chinese bbq sandwich*

To try to tell the whole wacky story of Mission Chinese Food would take up most of this blurb, so I'm going to whittle it down to this. Two guys take over the kitchen of an old-school Chinese restaurant and start doing pop-up dinners and they eventually take over the place and everybody in the food world goes ga-ga. There it is in a nutshell. Here's my two cents—these days it's hard to find interesting Chinese food in SF. Hard to believe, but true. So seeing and tasting how Danny and Anthony mash up Chinese and Korean and Vietnamese and Oklahoman (yes, you read that right) influences is a hoot and holler. Most of it works really well, some of it verges on a hot mess—but I'll take this anyday over mushy sweet and sour chicken.

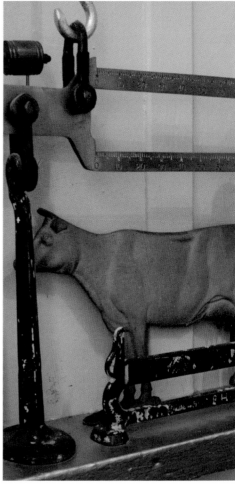

Why are cookbooks so seductive? Let me rephrase that question. Why aren't there more great cookbook stores? Answer to question one: because they are about food, and food is the ultimate seduction. Answer to question two: I have absolutely no idea, but thank goodness Celia Sack opened the wonderful, verging on perfection (I'm trying to think what the flaw is but can't come up with anything) **Omnivore Books**. If you love food and love to cook, then this little spot will bedazzle you. Or if you are like me and are attracted to pretty pictures married with well-written prose, then again, thank you Celia.

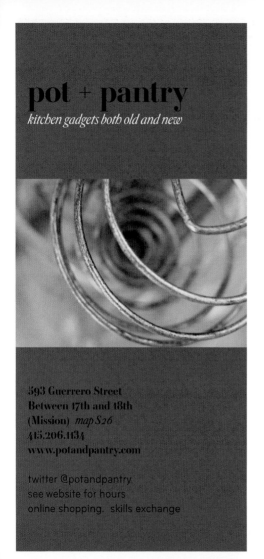

pot + pantry
kitchen gadgets both old and new

593 Guerrero Street
Between 17th and 18th
(Mission) *map S26*
415.206.1134
www.potandpantry.com

twitter @potandpantry
see website for hours
online shopping. skills exchange

Yes, Please: *the heated dishclothes, inna jam, sightglass coffee, gently used kitchenware, wade ceramics, vintage pyrex, mixing bowls, vintage mezzalunas*

Dear Donna, owner of Pot + Pantry, you made me lust for the vintage cast iron Le Creuset bean pot. There it was on your super darn cute blog in its round yellow glory. And then, just like that, I go to the shopping cart and I see the dreaded word SOLD next to the picture of the pot. Heartbreak. The only way to get over this is to spend more time visiting your cozy little bricks and mortar store. In fact, maybe if I stay here long enough you will uncover another one of those great pots, or I could console myself with any number of other vintage pieces of cookware or a perky dish towel. Actually, jam makes me happy, so I'll buy a couple of jars. Now I'm feeling better.

press: works on paper

never enough paper

3492 22nd Street
Corner of Dolores (Noe Valley) *map S27*
415.913.7156
www.pressworksonpaper.com

twitter @pressworkspaper
mon - sat 11a - 7p sun noon - 6p
online shopping. classes

Yes, Please: *"native funk & flash" by alexandra jacopetti,*
" hardcore crafts" by nancy bruning levine, brown duller
croquis, cubist erasers, japanese sewing scissors

I love paper. I could stop with that statement, but I've got some more to say about **Press: Works on Paper**. To begin with, many of the objects sold here are made of paper (or cut paper or write on paper). **PWOP** is one of those places where designey, paper-obsessed types like myself walk around and act a bit off—rustling pages of vintage magazines, sticking our noses right into the spine of out-of-print fashion books to catch a whiff of ink. Thankfully Nick Sarno and his wife Paulina are used to this type of behavior because they are also BOPPLs (big ole paper / print lovers). Hence why they opened a lovely spot for all of us with this affliction to spend our paper dollars at.

taylor stitch

custom tailored shirts and more

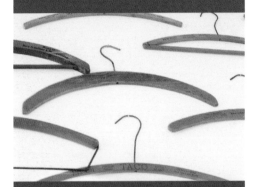

383 Valencia Street (at The Common)
Between 14th and 15th (Mission) *map S28*
415.322.8773
www.taylorstitch.com

twitter @taylorstitch
tue - sun 11a - 7p
online shopping. custom orders / design

Yes, Please: *jack style: charcoal striped rugby oxford, blue and green madras; pullover style: railroad stripe; california style: red bonfire plaid, peach and mint madras*

Every year my husband travels to Italy for business. And every year he returns looking like a tailored Italian male, sporting a sharp button-down worn under a soft cashmere sweater. I love this look and need to convince him to adopt it on a daily basis. I'll make my case by introducing him to **Taylor Stitch** shirts. All of the **TS** shirts are handmade in SF in limited quantities which means if you see something you like at their shop within a shop at **The Common**, you best grab it and run (please remember to pay). And if you'd prefer that red pinstripe you see in swatch form on the wall? Yes indeed, that can be custom made into a shirt for you—just take a moment to get measured and choose any number of stylistic options. In a month or so, you'll have shirt in hand.

the curiosity shoppe

*crafts, kits and curios for the
creatively inclined*

855 Valencia Street
Between 19th and 20th (Mission) *map S29*
415.671.5384
www.curiosityshoppeonline.com

twitter @cshoppe
tue - sat noon - 7p
sun noon - 6p
online shopping

Yes, Please: *jacqueline dufresne apple jacket,
sighn "its okay," katarina häl poem cup & saucer, ukulele
kit, "a field guide to weeds" by kim beck*

Though I may well be running out of interesting things to say as I get further into the writing this book, I could never run out of things to say about **The Curiosity Shoppe**. The happiest place on earth comes to mind (sorry Disneyland) whenever I step foot in here. What sets off my feel good bells? It's the goodies that owners Derek and Lauren choose. As you explore here, you'll see that there are lots of artistically driven, small-run or hand-crafted items, many of them with a cheeky sense of humor lodged into their DNA. You'll find yourself exploring here chuckling all the while. See? This is a happy making place!

tradesmen

vintage furnishings to lust for

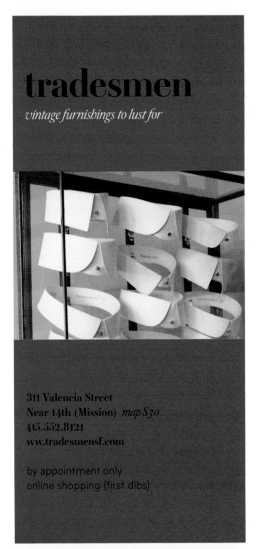

311 Valencia Street
Near 14th (Mission) *map S30*
415.552.8121
www.tradesmensf.com

by appointment only
online shopping (first dibs)

Yes. Please: *milo baughman burled olive loveseat, safe light, haberdashery collar display, machine age deco copper "covelite," painted advertising barrels*

I've always thought of Tradesmen like Willy Wonka's chocolate factory. A place where nobody went in and nobody came out. I have glued my face against the window here for the last six years in hopes that somebody, anybody, would appear to open the gates of this little kingdom of vintage goodness. Sadly, nobody came. I suspect there's an indentation in the glass, I've pressed my nose against it for so long. And then a Mission miracle happened. The door opened for me. Angels wept. Now that I've entered **Tradesmen** and touched the beauty within, I am complete.

unionmade

american and european heritage brands

493 Sanchez Street
Corner of 18th (Noe Valley) *map S31*
415.861.3373
www.unionmadegoods.com

twitter @unionmadegoods
mon - fri noon - 7p sat 11a - 7p
sun noon - 6p
online shopping

Yes, Please: *unionmade indigo golden bear pea coat, levi's vintage, nigel cabourn fair isle vest, alden, chester wallace, fox river red heel socks, juniper ridge, sns herning, filson*

I am a child of the '70s, and though I experimented with wearing Calvin Kleins and San Francisco Riding Gear, I believe with absolute certainty that Levi's are godhead when it comes to jeans. I take this belief so seriously it brought down a couple of boyfriends who didn't own a pair. And because I believe in these American heritage brands, I can advocate wholeheartedly for **Unionmade**. Owner Todd Barket, who might be one of the ten friendliest people on earth, has created a retail environment for men that carries a stellar collection of these goods. Just makes me wish I were a boy.

oakland

piedmont, lower hills, alameda

eat

shop

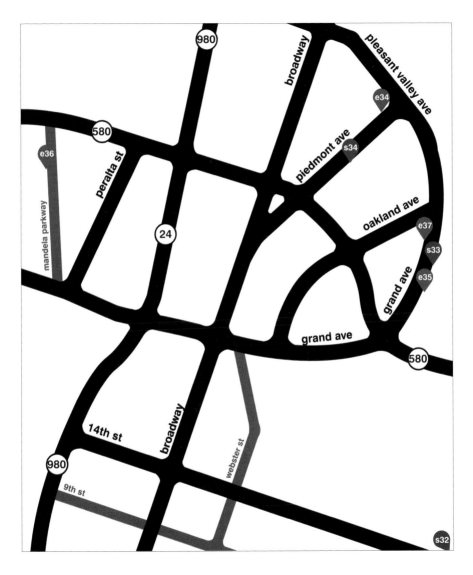

adesso

*house-cured meats and a hoppin'
aperitivo scene*

4395 Piedmont Avenue
Corner of Pleasant Valley
(Piedmont) *map E34*
510.601.0305
www.dopoadesso.com

mon - wed 5p - midnight
thu - sat 5p - 1a
dinner
$$ first come, first served

Yes. Please: *blood orange smash, 07 etna rosso,
firriato, sicilia, endless list of house-cured salumi, duck liver
in scatola pâté, arancini of pork ragu*

I know there's a big world of happy hours out there, but I can't bring myself to partake in them because I have a lurking fear of chafing dishes and half-warmed potato skins sprinkled with bac-o-bits. Then there's the *aperitivo* at **Adesso**. This I can embrace, as does a good chunk of Oakland it seems, judging by the packed house. The *aperitivo* is an Italian style happy hour, where you buy the drinks and **Adesso** provides heaping platters of finger foods, including their in-house cured salumi. Italians think the *aperitivo* stimulates the appetite for your dinner... sounds good to me.

boot and shoe service

sibling rivalry creates great pizza

3308 Grand Avenue
Between 580 and Mandana Boulevard
(Lower Hills) *map E35*
510.763.2668
www.bootandshoeservice.com

tue - thu 5:30 - 10p fri - sat 5 - 10:30p
sun 5 - 10p
dinner
$$ first come, first served

Yes, Please: *the salty witch, smoking lillies, crudo of fluke with avocado & watermelon radish, fritto misto of asparagus, onion & fennel, margherita pizza*

I know a whole bunch of adults who still have inferiority complexes in conjunction to their older sibling. What's up with that? I'd bet my last dollar that this isn't going to be an issue with **Boot and Shoe Service**, the latest offspring of Charlie Holliwell, whose first spot **Pizzaiolo** is worshipped in the East Bay. If anything, **BSS** is giving its sib a run for its money, as the place is packed from the moment the doors open. The pizza has a darn good char and the toppings are fresh and seasonal. Even if the name is a bit goofy (like calling your kid Moon Unit), this sibling has got it going on.

brown sugar kitchen

new style, down-home cooking

2534 Mandela Parkway
At 26th (Oakland) *map E36*
510.839.7685 (SOUL)
www.brownsugarkitchen.com

twitter @brownsugarkitch
tue - sat 7a - 3p sun 8a - 3p
breakfast. lunch
$-$$ first come, first served

Yes, Please: *brown sugar blend coffee, apple cider syrup, beignets & handmade jam, cornmeal waffle with brown sugar butter, fried oyster po-boy, sweet potato pie*

On the morning I took these pictures my first waking thought was, "I'm going to Brown Sugar Kitchen this morning." My wake up routine, which is usually blurry and slow at best, more resembled Usain Bolt heading for the shower. I was on the Bay Bridge in 20 minutes flat and sitting at the counter here 10 minutes after that. Five minutes later I had my order in for cheese grits with poached eggs AND a waffle. 20 minutes later I was rubbing my full belly, feeling like the day had started on a supremely good note. **Brown Sugar Kitchen** done me good.

camino

a wood-oven wonderland

3917 Grand Avenue
At Boulevard Way (Oakland) *map E37*
510.547.5035
www.caminorestaurant.com

twitter @caminooakland
dinner mon, wed - sun 5:30 - 10p
brunch sat - sun 10a - 2p
$$ reservations recommended

Yes, Please: *tequila blanco, cherry brandy, lime, grapefruit; local sardines with mashed garbanzo beans, asparagus with black trumpet mushrooms & egg*

Is it inappropriate to bring up fetishes in this book? Maybe so, but I'll do it anyway. I have a wee bit of a cookie fetish and also the clichéd female shoe fetish. My husband's dirty little secret is that he deeply desires a wood-burning oven in the kitchen. When I walked into **Camino**, I knew this place would make him burn with envy. Owner and chef Russell Moore has not just one oven, but two, where he cooks about 99% of his menu. The smells of a veritable cornucopia of fresh vegetables and meats being cooked over an open flame are almost sinful.

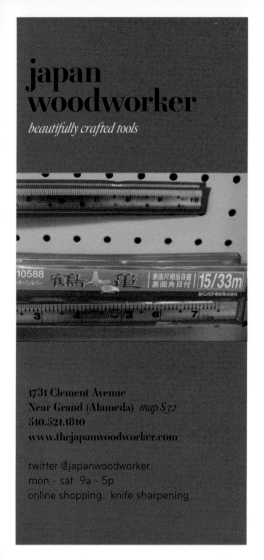

japan woodworker

beautifully crafted tools

1731 Clement Avenue
Near Grand (Alameda) *map S32*
510.521.1810
www.thejapanwoodworker.com

twitter @japanwoodworker
mon - sat 9a - 5p
online shopping. knife sharpening

Yes, Please: *shirogiku bonsai shears, charlie's soap, fein tools, tsunesaburo tamahagane smoothing plane , natural white nagura stone, yoshikane chef knife*

I like handcrafted tools, which is a bit kooky because I'm not really into the activities behind using these tools. For example, at **Japan Woodworker** there is a beautiful forest axe made by the Swedish company Gransfors Bruks. I would love to own this axe, but my pathetic arm strength wouldn't get it over my shoulder. No matter—I still covet it. After spending time wandering the aisles here with Jack, the resident knife sharpener and man of much knowledge, I had pipe dreams of making a kitchen table, carving a totem pole and becoming a sushi chef using tools found here. Just call me a dreamer.

mcmullen

pretty is as pretty does

1235 Grand Avenue
Near Fairview (Piedmont) *map S33*
510.658.6906
www.shopmcmullen.com

twitter @shopmcmullen
mon - sat 11a - 6p
sun noon - 5p
personal shopping alterations

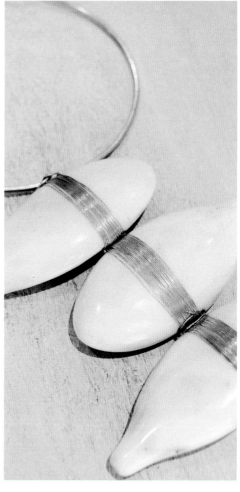

Yes, Please: *ports 1961, rag & bone, 3.1 phillip lim, vince, diane von furstenberg, by malene birger, loeffler randall, kingsley, souchi*

When I was little, even though I was a bit of a tomboy, I liked to dress up. When I moved to New York to go to college, I didn't wear a pair of jeans for four years. Today, though I spend most of my time hunched over a computer, I still love a good reason to wear pretty clothing. And when shopping for said lovelies, **McMullen** would be my first stop. Here I would find a cornucopia of dresses and other pieces that would fit the bill for everything from a dress to wear to work to an outfit for a night out on the town. And when I need to update my casual wardrobe, **McMullen** will also have some just right pieces.

mercy vintage now

well-edited vintage

4188 Piedmont
Corner Of Linda (Piedmont) *map S34*
510.654.5599
www.mercyvintage.com

twitter @mercyvintagenow
mon - sat 11a - 7p
sun 11a - 6p
online shopping

Yes, Please: *vintage: norma kamali, lilli diamond, courrèges, gaultier, qualicraft shoes; anna reutinger modified tees, elisa bongfeldt jewelry*

William Shakespeare wrote long ago, "Nothing emboldens sin so much as mercy." If sin be shopping, then yes, **Mercy Vintage Now** emboldens me on to do so. Owners Jenny and Karen have done a fantastic job turning this little corner space on Piedmont Ave. into a vintage clothing destination. They've chosen their collection well, ranging from high-end designer to '70s denim and everything in between. And because it's always a wise idea to mix up vintage with contemporary, there are some modern items like repurposed t-shirts thrown in for good measure. Mercy me.

berkeley

elmwood, rockridge, temescal (oakland)

eat

shop

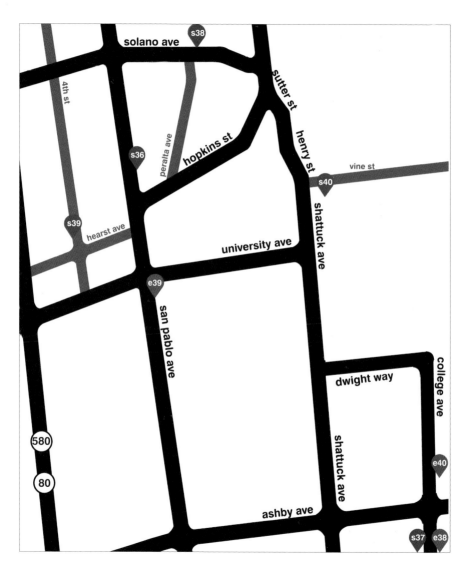

à côté

where substance trumps trend

5478 College Avenue
Between Lawton and Taft
(Rockridge) *map E38*
510.655.6469
www.acoterestaurant.com

twitter @acoterestaurant
sun – tue 5:30 – 10p wed – thu 5:30 – 11p
fri – sat 5:30 – midnight
dinner
$$ – $$$ reservations accepted

Yes, Please: *the vineyard cocktail, flor de anis cocktail, mussels with pernod, fig & pancetta flatbread, wood oven roasted game hen, ratatouille with lavender aioli*

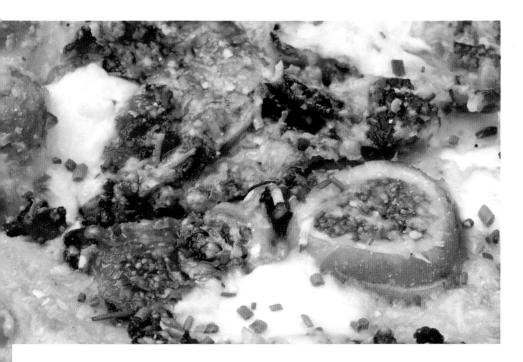

I get tired of hearing proclamations like "brown is the new black." Then blue is the new black and eventually black is the new black. Sometimes we get so caught up in what the hot new thing is, we overlook the things that are good day after day for years on end. À Côté is a prime example of this. Here you won't find taxidermied beasts hanging from the walls, rough hewn wood siding or a bearded waitstaff—what you will find is is the type of place where the bartender knows your name, has memorized your drink of choice and has been to your kids' graduations. And there's the food—it will leave you immensely satisfied and wanting more. Which is why you'll come back over and over again.

esqueleto

natural wonders

482a 49th Street - Temescal Alley
Corner of Telegraph (Temescal) *map S35*
212.920.5666
www.shopesqueleto.com

tue - sat noon - 6p
online shopping. custom orders / design

Yes, Please: *lauren wolf zeolite rings, all for the mountain scarves, len carella ceramics, bella bigsby prints, sarah swell, t. kahres, rebecca overmann, jessica winzelberg*

My mother tells me that when I was a child I had a habit of eating rocks. Eventually I grew out of it, grew up and became a mother to a daughter who also had an early taste for rocks. Thankfully she's moved beyond the pica phase, but we both continue to be fascinated by mineral nuggets. Imagine then my attraction to the jewelry at **Esqueleto** as I gazed at everything from necklaces to earrings and rings featuring a multitude of glorious rocks. Lauren Wolf, jeweler extraordinaire, embraces nature's themes in her pieces and also features other designers' work that complements this vision. Of course, I walked out with a pair of Lauren's pyrite stud earrings that I'm happy to tell you are firmly attached to my ears as they should be.

local 123

good coffee and more

2049 San Pablo Avenue
Between University and Addison
(Berkeley) *map E39*
415.517.8694
www.local123cafe.com

twitter @local123cafe
mon - fri 7a - 7p
sat - sun 7a - 5p
coffee /tea / wine. light meals. treats
$ first come, first served

Yes, Please: *coava chemex cone brew, flying goat coffee, mumbai chai, bionade, rosemary cheddar scone, sandwiches: the eggman, the walrus, salty goat*

Growing up in Portland, Oregon, I had a certain vision of Berkeley which included hippies, Alice Waters and people hanging out in coffee shops reading important pieces of literature. I've come to see over the years that this vision might be slightly askew, though Berkelites do like a mellow place to take a load off and sip a good cup of brew or a glass of wine. **Local 123** is the perfect example of this, and the locals are embracing it. Not only are they serving Healdsburg-based Flying Goat coffee, they are also making some tasty sustenance. All told, a very Berkeley sort of place.

oak barrel winecraft

beer and winemaking supplies

1443 San Pablo Avenue
Corner of Page (Berkeley) *map S36*
510.849.0400
www.oakbarrel.com

mon - fri 10a - 6p
sat 10a - 5p
online shopping. classes

Yes. Please: *hops: mt. hood, styrian golding, hallerteur; british porter kit, vinegar making kit, sake homebrew kit, grape listings, casks*

Not long after meeting my husband, I joined him in Barbaresco, Italy to take part in the grape harvest. We spent a couple of weeks having a blast working at friends' vineyards, eating great food and, yes, drinking some spectacular wine. Other than the Cabernet grapes, which were a pain in the ass to pick, the whole experience was amazing—so much so that I began to harbor a wee fantasy about making wine. And I could have gotten everything I needed at **Oak Barrel Winecraft**, right down to the grapes and also the fixings for beer, sake and vinegar making. Must get on this.

talisman antiques

the good stuff

6007 College Avenue
Near Harwood (Elmwood) *map S37*
510.653.7998

wed - sat 11a - 6p sun noon - 5p

Yes, Please: *19th century dough bowls, ikebana basket, early american overshot coverlets, 19th century native american feather basket, talivera ceramics*

One of the pluses of this job is that I get to see some of the most beautiful and unique retail environments in the country. In doing so, it's easy to see a theme emerge, and these days the popular retail story involves using American heritage objects as decorative elements. From Navajo rugs to washboards from the early 1900s, the past is hot. Enter **Talisman Antiques**, which has quietly been in business for 20 years selling what's now in vogue. You can find Kingsley Moore, the knowledgeable owner, refinishing pieces of cherry-picked early American furniture on the sidewalk, an image that bodes well for what lies inside. This is a place concerned not with trend, but with lovingly chosen objects, the history and provenance of which Kingsley can tell you down to the smallest detail. Beautiful.

the bone room

a natural history store

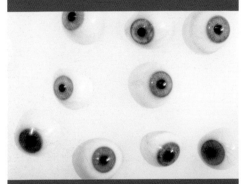

1569 Solano Avenue
Near Peralta (Berkeley) *map S38*
510.526.5252
www.boneroom.com
www.boneroompresents.com

twitter @boneroom
tue - wed, sat 11a - 6p. thu 11a - 9p.
online shopping. classes. rentals.
events / gallery at the bone room presents

Yes. Please: *raccoon tails, goliath beetles, giant marshall islands clam, "stiff" by marcy roach, dinosaur coprolites, budget skeletons, genuine spider webs*

Though my birthday gift wish list as a kid did not include a thorny devil stick framed in a shadow box, I've come to love taxidermy. Though some might find stuffing and preserving dead things somewhat macabre and Joel-Peter Witkinesque, I'm too prudish to get all wrapped up in the dark side. I just like natural history, and **The Bone Room**, in all its quirky glory, embraces just that. Owner Ron Cauble is the one of those über-smart Homo sapiens who should be able to be checked out at the library. He'll happily engage and teach everybody from school kids buying their first fossil to serious collectors looking for ancient hyena skulls. *Gratia*, Ron.

the gardener

beautiful things for the home & garden

1836 Fourth Street
Near Hearst (Berkeley) *map S39*
1 Ferry Building
EndoOf Market (Embarcadero)
East Bay 510.548.4545 / SF 415.981.8181
www.thegardener.com

see website for hours.
registries. classes

Yes, Please: *franchi seeds, alessi watering can, mango wood plates, fermob outdoor furniture, lilith rockett pottery, inna jam, vintage kantha pillows, cookbooks galore!*

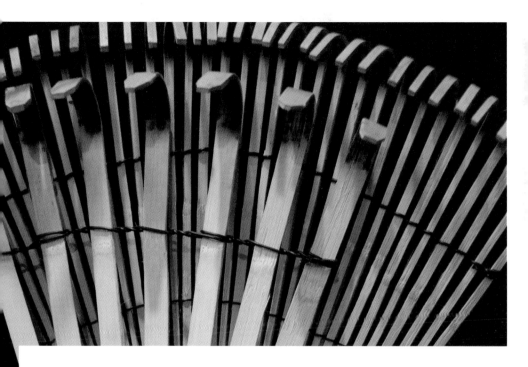

I really do (someday) want to garden. The thought of it is incredibly appealing, but every time I gaze at my parking strip with its carefully cultivated urban blend of weeds, I get discouraged. Coming to **The Gardener** does inspire me to buck up, spread some seeds and get dirty. This is an alluring place, not just for the items that inspired the name, but all of the other carefully sourced home and lifestyle pieces. I now have aspirations beyond the outdoors thanks to **The Gardener**, like wearing Zaya's metallic leather cuffs while weeding.

twig & fig

inspired letterpress designs

2110 Vine Street
Between Shattuck and Walnut
(Berkeley) *map S40*
510.848.5599
www.twigandfig.com

twitter @twigandfig
mon - sat 10a - 6p
custom design / orders

Yes, Please: *twig & fig: couture invitations, stationery, calling cards; penkridge porcelain fruit, screech owl design cards, caran d'ache pens*

About 15 years ago, I had a hot case of letterpress lust. I had a line on a couple of vintage Heidelbergs and an idea for a studio. But life intervened, and my letterpress dreams went by the wayside. To this day, I can't be around this craft without getting weak-kneed, which is what happened at **Twig & Fig**. Suzie and Serge are a formidable creative team and make the most outrageously detailed custom invites and accompanying collateral I've ever seen, which brought on some serious designer envy. But I got over it so I could browse the paperie, which has a swell selection of paper goods and lifestyle goodies.

vintage berkeley

affordable artisanal wines

2949 College Avenue
Between Ashby and Russell
(Berkeley), *map E40*
510.549.9501
www.vintageberkeley.com

twitter @vintageberkeley
see website for hours and other locations
wine shop
$-$$ first come, first served

Yes, Please: *cava avinyo brut reserva nv, penedes; 09 cep (peay vineyards) rose, sonoma coast; 08 gulfi rossojbleo nero d'avola, sicily; vina do burato ribeira sacra*

I have a chequered history with wine. My first memories of the grape came in the form of the boxed wines of the '80s, consumed by my parents on ski trips. Then there was the Annie Green Springs varietal (lemon satin country cherry, anyone?) that popped up in college. Against all odds, I married into a family that sells wine for a living. Ten years later I'm still learning, but I can spot a great wine shop, and **Vintage Berkeley** fits the bill. At their striking retail spaces, you can find an eclectic array of wines, most under $25, from around the world. You'll never consider Two Buck Chuck again.

etc.

studio only, no storefronts

shop

basil racuk
nomade exquis
story boxes

notes

basil racuk

custom leather bags and accessories

510.409.4452
www.basilracuk.com

twitter @basilracuk
by appointment only
custom design / orders

Yes, Please: *basil racuk leather goods: weekender travel bag, hard brief, suspension belt, computer case, farmer's market tote, sling purse, soft brief*

Many years ago my mother and I purchased a beautiful leather shoulder bag together. We have passed it back and forth ever since. But when I buy one of **Basil Racuk's** bags, all of my childhood lessons about sharing are going out the window. Sorry Mom—these custom-made, handcrafted bags demand to be hoarded. Basil, whose design chops have been honed at some iconic American brands, clearly knows his way around a piece of leather. What makes his work so desirable is that it's not machine-made perfect, but full of that handmade quality that signifies a piece of art.

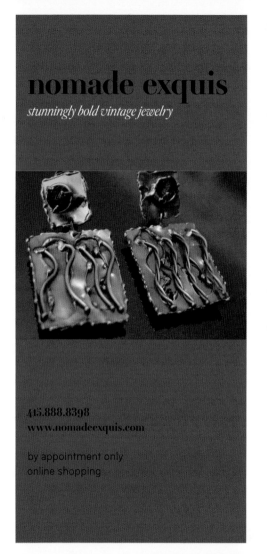

nomade exquis

stunningly bold vintage jewelry

415.888.8398
www.nomadeexquis.com

by appointment only
online shopping

Yes, Please: *robert larin, ernendes, guy vidal, alfred karram, jorma laine, betty cooke, pentti sarpaneva, de passille-sylvestre*

I'm studying the striking business card for Nomade Exquis. It's the image of a woman's naked upper torso wearing a bold exclamation point of a necklace. It's the perfect image for the stunning vintage jewelry that owner Mo Clancy sells. Many of these pieces are incredibly powerful and can stand alone as an artistic statement, but when they interact with the curves of a human body, they come alive. Even if your taste runs to more classical or delicate body adornments, you'll find it hard not to be drawn to the strength of this jewelry. When I slipped a bracelet on I felt like Athena—empowered and bold.

story boxes

elaborate, heirloom quality story and shadow boxes

415.221.2682
www.juliehaas.com

by appointment only
cash only. custom design / orders

Yes, Please: *custom designed: story boxes, shadow boxes*

There I was scouring the mean streets of Presidio Heights, when I saw a window display next to a dry cleaners, which held an exquisitely ornate box. There was a calligraphed note that said **Story Boxes** and a phone number. I was hooked. But where was this **Story Boxes** store? Was it in the back of the dry cleaners? Turns out there is no store. Just Julie Haas making both story and shadow boxes to order, using your stories and treasured mementos as well as her talent and vast supply of artistic materials. Take note—these are heirloom quality pieces and are priced as such. But they are worth every penny.

finito

happy travels to you

rather *san francisco*

isbn-13 9780984425396

copyright 2011 ©swiftrank. printed in the usa

every effort has been made to ensure the accuracy of the information in this book. however, certain details are subject to change. please remember when using the guides that hours alter seasonally and sometimes sadly, businesses close. the publisher cannot accept responsibility for any consequences arising from the use of this book.

editing / fact checking + production: chloe fields
in design master: nicole conant
map design + production: julia dickey + bryan wolf

thx to our friends at designers & agents for their hospitality and their support of the rather experience. please visit > designersandagents.com

rather is distributed by
independent publishers group > www.ipgbook.com

to peer further into the world of **rather** and to buy books, please visit **rather.com** to learn more